CW00924879

A Life Drawing
FROM CORN RICKS TO COMIC STRIPS

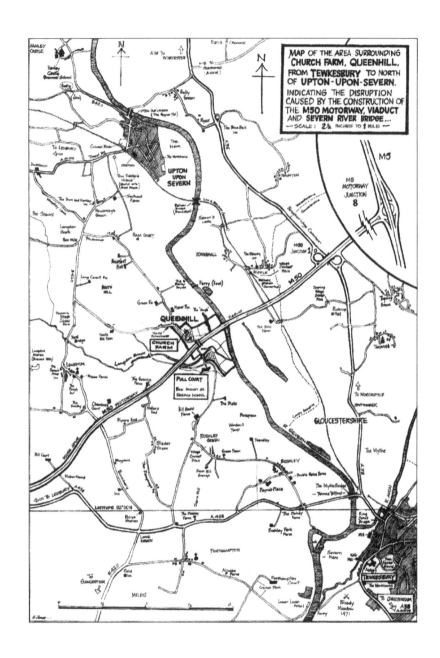

MAP OF THE AREA SURROUNDING CHURCH FARM, QUEENHILL, FROM TEWKESBURY TO NORTH OF UPTON-UPON-SEVERN. INDICATING THE DISRUPTION CAUSED BY THE CONSTRUCTION OF THE M50 MOTORWAY, VIADUCT AND SEVERN RIVER BRIDGE... — SCALE: 2½ INCHES TO 1 MILE —

A Life Drawing

FROM CORN RICKS TO COMIC STRIPS

Geoff Jones

BANK HOUSE BOOKS

Some material published in the United Kingdom in 2007 by
The Cider Apple Press

This edition published in 2008 by
Bank House Books
BIC House
1 Christopher Road
East Grinstead
West Sussex RH19 3BT

BANK HOUSE BOOKS is a division of BANK HOUSE MEDIA Ltd

British Library Cataloguing in Publication Data
A catalogue record for this book is available from the British
Library.

ISBN 9781904408369

Typesetting and origination by Bank House Books
Printed and bound by Lightning Source.

Chapter One

Spring had arrived early in the troubled year of 1940, and by mid-May the farmland of the Severn Valley was already lush and verdant. A few weeks away from my eleventh birthday, I had acquired a deep affection for the farm that had always been the centre of my existence. The picturesque farmhouse and buildings nestled in a south-facing hollow. Behind the homestead the land rose quite steeply into a ridge that served as a rampart, sheltering us from the icy northern blasts of winter. This barrier had always seemed to be a natural protection against any adverse happening, a comforting shield.

The house and building were almost surrounded by an apple orchard, which in springtime became a riot of colour and added an extra element to the attraction of it all. The farmhouse, like so many in the region, was a miscellany of many styles. It had been enlarged many times since the basic shelter had arisen several centuries before. The original portion was half-timbered and had been built, as was the norm, around an enormous chimney. Apparently, all those years ago, if a chimney was built in a day and smoke emitted from it before nightfall, it was possible to claim all the land around to a certain distance. Whether that is true is open to doubt, but it's what the legend says. It certainly was a very large chimney. At the base it was like a small room: it was possible to stand inside and look up the tapering brickwork to the large square of sky visible at the top.

The rest of the house seemed to have been attached at different stages in its evolution. A large cellar lay underneath the original portion. There were two separate flights of stairs in different parts of the dwelling; one was quite a majestic affair. Everywhere had large stone slabs, which contrary to modern fashionable opinion were actually cold and uninviting. In winter especially they were always clammy and damp, sometimes even visibly wet.

To the south the land dropped away through strangely ornamental parkland, to the rich alluvial grassland beside the Severn itself. These uplands had been planted with various exotic trees, mainly sequoias, but also some unusual eastern Mediterranean species, varieties of cork oaks and cedar. The Dowdeswells had owned the Pull Court Estate for many years, and like so many landowning families in the nineteenth century they had produced at least one son who had travelled the world as a plant collector. Church Farm had been, in effect, the home farm of the estate, so it was no surprise that they had chosen to plant their imported and rare specimens within its fields.

The river flooded often, but only in the winter months. The floods would cover roughly half of the farm but the house buildings were a hundred feet higher than the floodplain and were mercifully in no danger of inundation.

Tradition has it that Edward IV's Queen watched one of the major battles in the War of the Roses, which took place at Tewkesbury in 1471, from the summit of the hill here. They named the hill after her, but it all seems pretty fanciful; even to my young mind it seemed scarcely credible. The scene of the bloodshed lay at least five miles away to the south and over the other side of the Severn. I remember deciding that she must have possessed remarkably acute eyesight.

Looking south, the pale blue silhouette of Tewkesbury Abbey was clearly visible above the distant trees and was strangely reassuring in its permanence. Beyond and around to the east, behind the familiar tump of A.E. Housman's beloved Bredon Hill, lay the long line of the west-facing Cotswold escarpment.

To the west, across what had once been a royal hunting forest, the unique ridge of the Malvern Hills rose abruptly, unusually blue and distant in the warmth of early summer. Even further in the distance lay further ridges, all individually recognisable to my retentive and enquiring young mind. First was the ridge below Ross-on-Wye, then the Black Mountains and Brecon Beacons. To the south, well to the west of the abbey, lay May Hill, with its clump of trees perched like a tiny hat on the familiar dome which rises above the Forest of Dean.

All around lay remnants, the pathetic reminders of the previous day's farm sale. The familiar implements had been laid out in rows, then prodded and kicked by the hordes of inquisitive locals who had descended like vultures looking for bargains.

All the dairy shorthorns, which I'd grown to know as permanent fixtures, had been corralled into a temporary enclosure.

Amid much bellowing and nervous ejections of hosepiping excrement they had been sold, thwacked mercilessly by strangers with long ash sticks, and had disappeared forever.

Cattle Dealer.
(end of book)

The same went for the sheep, pigs, fowls and the two Suffolk Punch carthorses. This was the pre-tractor era. They'd all suddenly gone and the fields were empty: the yards and looseboxes held nothing but memories. But after what had happened in the preceding six weeks this was yet another mind-numbing shock to the system. What next, I wondered?

Now, more than sixty years later, all that happened at that time remains crystal clear in my mind. The day after Hitler's troops flooded into Norway dawned just like any other day. But suddenly the world changed, and pandemonium reigned.

I remember it all so clearly. First the bloodcurdling screams, the realisation that something awful had befallen somebody. We soon realised that our much revered father, the kingpin of our little isolated world, had been killed in an accident on the farm. Before long the place was teeming with people. I do not remember panicking, even at that tender age. I felt a great need to remain calm and not to disintegrate.

Somehow each sleepless day merged into the next. I was always grateful that my brother and I were not dragged off to the funeral. Well-meaning relatives put their arms around my shoulders and said strangely unbelievable things like 'it's up to you to look after your mother now'. I was ten years old!

I have a particularly clear memory of what happened two or three weeks later, when the summer term started at school. I was already a pupil at Hanley Castle Grammar School, which entailed cycling five miles each way every day. The day arrived on which I began this daily marathon once again, and I found myself cycling alone along the well-known rutted lanes and on through the small local market town of Upton upon Severn. About half a mile from my destination I heard the school bell start to ring. I could see the familiar brick red building ahead. Suddenly I turned round and cycled quietly home.

Nobody chided me when I returned. I think they felt pity, but who knows. The next day I made it all the way to school. Everybody was very kind and murmured quiet words of understanding. I don't really remember crying very much at anything that happened in those weeks; it was somehow more awful than that.

During May and June of that year ominous things had been going on in Northern France and in the English Channel. My father kept us informed of what was happening on the world stage. Christened Vivian George Jones, he had managed to survive four years on the Western Front during the madness of the First World War. Here we were, just over twenty years later, once again at war with the same country. I remember listening to the radio to descriptions of Hitler entering Czechoslovakia, of Munich and Chamberlain's visit. All this interspersed with Len Hutton's 364 at The Oval against Australia in 1938. Then one Sunday morning we listened as a family, in the little room with the telephone and the roll-top desk, to the sombre announcement by Chamberlain that as he had not heard from Hitler by eleven o'clock we were now at war with Germany.

Late spring merged into high summer. Our farm was eventually let to a tenant from across the border in the principality to the west. My mother, brother and I moved from the now empty farm to Hanley Swan, a village some seven or eight miles away, close to the Malvern Hills.

9

Dunkirk had happened, and everybody seemed to be expecting an invasion by German paratroopers at any time. The sky was full of aircraft, but the roads almost empty of traffic – apart from army lorries chasing frantically about the place. (The roads were so empty that us lads even perfected the art of riding bikes 'backwards' – sitting on the handlebars – for miles!)

So much had changed in my young life in such a short time.

Chapter Two

The next four years were dominated by the overwhelming threat of being at war and by school. The land between Hanley Swan and the Malverns was suddenly transferred into an enormous military camp. What had been the picturesque Blackmore Park was now a sea of brick huts and interconnecting roads. In the year in which the construction took place, hordes of Hibernian workmen appeared and on the extra long summer evenings, for there was now double summer time and daylight until past eleven o'clock, I could lean out of the bedroom window and hear ethereal singing as these men returned from the local pub to their communal quarters, way up back in the woods. Beautiful crystal clear voices would ring into the night air with harmonies of surprising quality, as the homesick workers sang 'Galway Bay' and many other songs of County Mayo and beyond.

Then suddenly came the infamy of Pearl Harbor, and before long there were American troops in the newly built camp. They also would come down to the local pub in the evening and sit out on the village green under a large oak tree. There was even a picture postcard village pond on which we all slid in wintertime.

11

Many of the young Americans were not much older than we were and seemed to want to talk about the land they had left behind. The war had educated my generation geographically, with daily maps in the newspapers of all the battlegrounds of the moment.

One incident from those wartime years, when we were surrounded by American soldiers but rural life continued, with the village green as the hub of our adolescent lives, remains clearly and indelibly stamped on my brain. I think it may have been influential in shaping my attitude towards those people in this life who misuse their delegated power. We'd been playing football on the village green, but as twilight approached we retired to the area surrounding the enormous oak tree to talk. A single figure approached our little group. He was dressed in an American army uniform, and was carrying a guitar slung over his shoulders. He sat down on the grass alone, about twenty yards from us, and began to play. It's difficult to believe it, but this was the first time I'd ever heard a guitar played. The music was extremely haunting and beautiful. By now we had all moved forward and just sat and listened. Nobody said a word. We could see that he was either a Native American or a Mexican.

After a lot of unaccompanied guitar picking, he began to sing what were obviously songs of the land beyond the Rio Grande. There was a popular song of that era, originally popularised by Gene Autry, called 'I'm dreaming tonight of my blue eyes'. Merely playing this tune seemed to affect him deeply. He was probably wishing he was back in his land with his chosen senorita – or anywhere other than in a foreign land, about to be thrown into a dangerous conflict not of his own making.

Suddenly we were aware of the arrival at great speed, with much revving of engines and shouting, of a US Army Jeep containing four enormous bull-necked military policemen in white helmets. Screaming obscenities, they fell on the poor and harmless minstrel. The most repeated phrase seemed to be 'f—ing wet back'. He *was* a Mexican, apparently. They hurled him into the Jeep and gave him a really severe beating up. Then they turned their attention to his guitar, which they jumped on and smashed to fragments, kicking it into a nearby hedge.

Some of us approached these pathetic thugs and asked them what they thought they were doing, which probably wasn't a clever move. The reaction was predictable. I remember a shaven-headed Neanderthal a few inches from my nose, telling me in very precise and obscene words just what I could do about it.

This type of degrading intolerance was still the norm in many parts of the southern States until well into the seventies.

*****

The war dominated our existence, and to this day the layout of the whole Pacific basin remains as clear as ever: places like Guadalcanal, Guam, Midway, Luzon, the Celebes were indelibly stamped on our young and receptive minds. Not that I felt war was anything other than appalling. There was certainly no glamour or excitement in it as far as I was concerned. What was to happen later confirmed my loathing of it all – even though the Second World War was necessary. Actually, it was probably the only war in the twentieth century that was justified and unavoidable. Fascism was an obscenity.

Soon came the expected news of the D-Day landings in Normandy. Almost immediately, practically on the evening of the very day, lines of Dodge ambulances began to go past our front gate with ever increasing regularity. Our cottage was between the local railway station and the hospital buildings back in the woods. For about thirty-six hours they came past slowly, nose to tail. It was obvious to us at least that they had suffered very heavy casualties on those beaches in Normandy. Listening to the radio you didn't get that idea at all, but some of the correspondents gave pretty graphic accounts and they couldn't drown the noise of battle.

After a few weeks some of the wounded began to make their way down to the pub on the village green. We knew about the realities of war but this was still a shock. Many of them were still in their teens; many had limbs missing. Quite a proportion seemed to have been blinded and were dependent on their colleagues, even to move about.

Probably the worst images that still inhabit my memory were of screaming shell-shocked patients being transported between the camps in large cages on the backs of the open trucks. One hapless character managed to escape from a camp and climbed an electricity pylon on one of my uncle's fields. There was apparently a large flash and a charred body at the base of the pylon. My uncle Henry had endured unspeakable hardships at the hands of the Turks as a POW in the First World War, but he never discussed it. He was extremely shaken by this event. To me it all contributed to a lifelong pacifism, a hatred of war, and a deep contempt for all who glorify war and all things military.

But the war was yet to end, and who knew what would then lie in store? We thought it might last another twenty years. Many local youths had already paid the ultimate price. For example, two brothers who lived almost opposite us were killed, one in North Africa and the other in Crete. Neither reached his twenty-first birthday. Their ageing and dignified parents both turned white haired in months.

Almost every night the skies were swarming with droning bombers. There was the easily identifiable burbling sound of the Junkers 88, which made windows rattle and searchlight beams scour the skies. Away to the north there was a nightly glow in the sky as bombs rained mercilessly on Birmingham and Coventry and their luckless inhabitants. It was obvious that the waves of bombers were following the River Severn, and later they would return. We were mercifully spared most of the bombing, although on occasions planes shed some of their cargo on the return journey. These bombs would usually fall harmlessly in open countryside, but sometimes there were civilian casualties. I remember seeing a stick of incendiaries fall, and the ensuing blaze, but events like this were few and far between.

A friend of mine,who used to live in this area, recently recalled an amazing tale about bombs being unloaded as the bombers headed home. It was midwinter and the Severn was in flood. Longdon Marsh, west of Hanley Swan towards the Malverns, had once more become a lake, as it had been until it was drained in the 1850s. In the light of the full moon our Teutonic friends thought the large trees protruding from the floodwater were ships – and dropped a whole batch of bombs thereupon. My friend also tells me that three or four miles to the west, at Berrow, there was a disguised airfield, with moveable 'hedges', from which Odette Churchill and other agents were flown to France. I'm not sure if I believe this.

One of the very few landmines to be dropped on Britain fell on my uncle's farmland. His buildings were left devoid of roof tiles, and his house needed fresh glass in every window.

We became experts at aircraft recognition. We could differentiate between a Fairey Battle and a Fairey Fulmar, Lancasters from Stirlings, Typhoons from Tornados. There were all sorts in the sky every day. North American Harvard trainers emitted a unique sound as they passed, a quick raucous rasp for a few seconds and then relative peace again. Spitfires hurtled about the skies with their distinctive note, which was not unlike tearing calico. There were also lots of biplanes: early on there were Gladiators, Swordfish and a great many Tiger Moth trainers engaging in mock dogfights. Lysanders sometimes appeared to be flying backwards. Later in the war De Havilland Mosquitos became quite a common sight, so sleek and manoeuvrable. Amazingly they were constructed of wood, we were told in some consternation.

Suddenly one day, probably in 1941, we were amazed by a small snub-nosed low-wing monoplane that had no propeller and was silent apart from a sort of conspiratorial whistle. We were stumped. What was it? Later we realised it was the prototype Gloster Jet Fighter, the E28/39, up on test flights from Brockworth: the first jet aircraft, Frank Whittle's amazing invention. We saw its first flights.

A few months before the war ended my mother remarried, and we moved back to the farm we had always thought of as home.

Chapter Three

Although it was with a feeling of elation that we returned to our rightful home, there were some considerable differences when we got back. My brother Mick had gone off to Bristol University to study agriculture, which left the three of us: my mother, my newly acquired stepfather and me. I certainly never felt any jealousy toward him, but neither did I feel any sort of affection, and neither did he toward me.

Going back to our farm also meant a return to living without mains electricity or mains water. We had become used to twentieth-century conveniences in the intervening four years. But it still felt wonderful to be home again, even though I quickly realised that I would be expected to do my fair share of everyday farming tasks, even if I was still at school.

Quite a common sight in my childhood

On a normal day I set off at eight o'clock to cycle the five miles to school, studied for what was then called school certificate (later O levels), and then made the wearying return cycle ride. Once home I was expected to quickly change into working clothes and make myself useful feeding calves, helping with afternoon milking, collecting eggs by the bucketful from the free-range poultry, feeding the many pigs in the Danish-style piggery and, indeed, doing anything else necessary. My first week back at the farm coincided with the first week of the school certificate exams. How on earth concentration on revision was possible I'll never know. During the whole two week exam period each evening and the weekend in between were devoted almost completely to haymaking till the daylight failed. Perhaps this was proof that last minute revision for exams is, if anything, counter productive and adds confusion; who knows? But by some strange quirk of fortune I did pretty well, especially as I was more than a year younger than the rest of the form.

Back at school that autumn I began sixth form studies. In those faraway days there were no career advisors, and nobody much cared what happened. The war was still on, and would possibly last for years, so the odds were that you would join the army, navy or the air force. That seemed to be the only choice open to any of us: cannon fodder.

But things changed in Northern Europe, and as the next summer arrived we were at peace in part of the world at least. Of course there was the Far Eastern conflict to conclude, and that didn't seem likely to happen for years. I suppose most of my contemporaries shared my dread that sooner or later we would find ourselves, unwillingly, on some Pacific island preparing to invade Japan itself. But suddenly there was news on the radio about atom bombs being dropped, and days later the war was over completely. At last. It had seemed unlikely ever to end: we'd known very little else.

It has always seemed to me that the allies were completely justified in bombing Hiroshima and Nagasaki. Who started it all anyway? Whose idea was world domination in the first place? The Germans and Japanese would have had no qualms about using atomic weapons if they had perfected them ahead of us, and apparently they were pretty close to acquiring them. I'm sure that the thousands of prisoners who died or suffered abominably at the hands of the Japanese would have had little difficulty in supporting Harry Truman's momentous decision. Those who came through the whole disgusting experience were, in so many cases, physically ruined beyond repair. Many of them, with yellowed skin and frail bodies, only lived a few years of freedom after 1945.

In the years before the war we'd grown accustomed to the cheery countenance of the appropriately named cowman, Wilf Bullock. He'd worked for my father since leaving school and was a mine of country knowledge. When the farm changed hands in 1940 he wasn't deemed necessary, and in no time he was yet another statistic in khaki. By January 1942 he was in Malaya. He must have been confused by what had happened to him. I doubt if, before being called up, he'd ever been further than Gloucester. But here he was, on the other side of the world, about to take on the might of Hirohito. Of course, like so many thousands of British troops, he was captured and spent years on the construction of the notorious Burma Railway. He survived, but only just. I saw him briefly when he came home. He was just a bag of bones, discoloured by repeated doses of malaria. He did at least die in peace in his beloved Worcestershire, but he was back among us for only a few months.

*****

I'd spent a year in the sixth form taking subjects that weren't going to benefit me in any way. Nobody really cared, it seemed to me. It was rather amazing that anybody learnt anything in the schools of wartime Britain. All the younger male teachers left to join the forces, and their female replacements were all, it seemed, straight from university – and had very little idea of how to pass on their skills to hordes of male students. They came and went with amazing rapidity. In four years I was taught French by seven different female teachers, which worked out at about one every two terms.

In retrospect I realise that very few useful skills were passed down to the following generation at this confused time in our history. Perhaps, in my case, it had something to do with not having the advantage of any form of paternal guidance. All of the agricultural skills I ever acquired were gained by observing what other people did. Certainly nobody taught me to drive. I watched other people driving tractors, and then suddenly it was me in charge of the potentially dangerous machine. Over a period of time you graduated to driving the farm Jeep, and eventually it was time for your driving test.

The first time I drove a car for any distance on the public road was my trip to Worcester to take my test. I hadn't got a car, and my stepfather would never have agreed to my driving his vehicle, so in January 1949 I took my test in an aged 1937 Hillman Minx which belonged to my brother.

This was incredibly over confident of me: I should have failed for I had never driven in city streets before. But luck was with me, it seemed, that luck taking the form of a puncture. During the test I was suddenly aware of a flat front tyre. I leapt out and, in a crowded street, quickly changed the wheel and nipped back behind the controls. The examiner seemed greatly impressed by this display of expertise, and on our return to the testing station wrote out a pass certificate! What luck indeed.

It was a rather similar situation with regard to sport. In wartime schools, even though ours was a grammar school, we had no coaching at either soccer or cricket. You read old pre-war manuals about forward defensive strokes and so on, but apart from that it was all down to common sense and observation.

I wasted a great deal of energy at football in my teens by dashing about as a centre forward, at full tilt for the full ninety minutes. Then my stepfather's brother Willie, who was as different from his close relative as chalk from cheese, confided a few of his own hard-earned observations. He was a remarkable man who had worked in every continent in the world as a civil engineer and also as a member of the Chinese customs on the Yangtse. He had spent practically all the war years in tankers on the North

Atlantic convoys. Being sunk on more than one occasion, he had once spent twelve days in an open lifeboat before being washed up on the Outer Hebrides. He had a graphic tale of being on a tanker on one of the infamous voyages to Murmansk that took ships all around the German-held coast of Norway. On this occasion a great sheet of ice removed most of the ship's superstructure, but they managed to limp into Archangel.

In his youth he had been apprenticed to the Austin Motor Company and had played soccer at quite a high level, culminating in a season as centre forward for Cardiff City. He must have seen my pathetic efforts at some stage because he suggested that it might be advantageous if I paced myself rather more shrewdly during the course of the ninety minutes. Subtle changes of pace at specific crucial incidents, such as avoiding lunging tackles, even risking a few minutes of apparent inactivity, would lull your opponents into over-confidence. That was the only piece of soccer coaching I ever received, but it turned out to be remarkably beneficial.

*****

That autumn I left school to work for my stepfather – also, rather confusingly, named Jones – Alan Jones. There had been quite a bit of pressure on me to do this but in retrospect it was a ghastly mistake. It wasn't so much a learning period, it was more a time of concentrated slavery. Most farmers' sons were taken occasionally to market to learn the value of livestock and were consulted about plans as to what to grow in various fields. In other words, they learned to be farmers. For me, though, the next five or six years were something of a nightmare. Work was never-ending, from shortly after six every morning to half past six in the evening. Weekends were almost as bad. Most people still worked a five and a half day week but cows had to be milked and livestock had to be fed on Saturday afternoons and Sundays too. Farming was indeed unique.

But I did stick to my guns in one respect. At school I'd done quite well as a footballer and as a cricketer. I was allowed, although certainly not encouraged, to play football for the local market town, Upton upon Severn, every Saturday. But on alternate Saturdays, when it was my turn to do the milking, this could entail riding the four miles home after a hard ninety minutes of football, not stopping to wash the mud off (in any case this would have been done with two or three buckets of communal cold water in a rustic shed), and working by lantern light till eight o'clock or later with about thirty cows. I grew to dislike cows as the years passed, and when that period of my life closed I never had any desire to tend to a herd of cows ever again.

Cricket was similar, but in summer it was less unpleasant to return to cows after a match. In those years club cricket was played (in our town anyway) only on Saturdays, not on Saturday and Sunday as became the norm later. It was apparently too sinful a pursuit to be indulged in on the Sabbath. As someone who has never believed in any supernatural deity, this ruling astounded me, but it was strictly adhered to. The humourless countenances representing the Lord's Day Observance Society held sway in their dark suits and with their melancholy utterances. I suppose the crimes of blasphemy and heresy were still in force too? Even then it seemed to be the height of conceit for anyone to claim that some benevolent supernatural force apparently up in the clouds had all their personal worries and troubles in hand. What about the other billions on the surface of the earth, as well as those that had gone before us for thousands of years? Somebody had their hands full up there, it seemed, for computers were a thing of the future.

Apparently before the industrial revolution there was no great feeling of work being a noble pursuit that was to be encouraged at any cost. This 'work ethic' became accepted as the norm at the behest of the mill owners and the coal mine moguls, as a method of recruiting labour, and was promoted by the Church. It's surely possible that all religions were concocted to enable the few to exert power over the many. Why can't people see this might be the case?

*****

In the autumn of 1946 we were hooked up to the national electricity grid. The change that this created was earth shattering. Before this great step forward, illumination around the farm buildings had relied on old farm lanterns, which were carried from task to task.

Apart from these little patches of light everywhere was pitch black. Sometimes the metal handles of the lanterns would squeak rhythmically as people walked about. It conjures up a scene from early spooky films – and it really was like that. The rambling farmhouse had been converted to calor gas by my father but only downstairs. When, as children, we went up the wide stairway to bed we held ancient candlesticks, and often read by candlelight until sleep overtook us.

It must have been quite dangerous, young children roaming about darkened rooms with naked flames, but people survived. In the scullery, by the back door, one of the lanterns was kept (alight until bedtime) on top of the ancient pump that supplied non-drinking water for household tasks. When anything happened outside, this lantern was grabbed and taken out into the icy blast. It  was also used to guide us in the hours of darkness to the small brick outhouse that lay at the bottom of the garden. Strangely this was not a very common need.

All drinking water came from a very deep well, a hundred yards away in a rickyard. There was still an old well and pump in the garden, concreted over and condemned as unfit for human consumption as it had been infiltrated by the roots of a yew tree, long since removed. One of the first tasks every day was to fetch water from the pump in the rickyard by means of a yoke, which you carried on your shoulders.

Carrying Drinking Water back to the farmhouse ...

From each end of this a large, lidded, galvanised bucket was suspended on chains. It was like a scene from the middle ages. Although the total weight on your shoulders was perhaps in excess of half a hundredweight, the two buckets balanced themselves so well that it was a comparatively easy task. The difficulty was in keeping your feet as you negotiated the muddy track back to the slippery brick steps that led down the equally slippery wet brick-paved yard outside the back door.

After morning milking and a hurried breakfast one of the necessary tasks every day was to spend about twenty minutes pumping water from the rickyard pump for the pigs, calves and bull. It was also used to wash up the milking buckets and cooler, and swill out the dairy. There was the usual small trough by the pump. From this a lead pipe led underground for about a hundred yards before emerging over a very large trough by the dairy. Like all such troughs at that time it was stone, probably six feet long, four feet deep and four feet wide. Its capacity was never calculated accurately, but was probably several hundred gallons. Even on the coldest day sweat would pour off you as you pumped. It was probably extremely beneficial to youthful muscle development – and the trough would no doubt be worth a fortune today as a garden design centrepiece.

Suddenly there was light everywhere, in each shed, sty, stable, granary and barn, even on tall poles in the centre of the cattle yard and on corners of buildings. There was a great temptation to leave them all on and enjoy the difference it made. It also dealt the death knell to candles at bedtime. No longer did we have to rely on stone hot water bottles to defeat the damp sheets so common in those rambling old farmhouses. In really wet weather the interior walls would run with damp. To anyone who had to endure the discomforts of an old farmhouse in that era, the squeals of delight emitting from trendy house decorators when they discover 'these lovely old flagstones' are difficult to comprehend. They were damp, uneven and very hard.

Chapter Four

ack in the days before combine harvesters became commonplace, when we still cut the cornfields' headlands with a 'hook and crook', one of the usual happenings of the winter months was the visit of the local contract-threshing operator.

This always seemed to take place in the very depths of winter, often immediately after Boxing Day. The contractor probably had a well-worn route, and it just happened that we came to associate threshing on our farm with snow. About half of the farm comprised floodable Severn river meadows, which was an advantage as far as grass yields were concerned, but had its disadvantages too. Hayricks couldn't be built in the field: each load had to be hauled up the steep tracks and built into ricks around the back of the cowsheds. My earliest memories are of wooden-wheeled wagons as used in Victorian times, being hauled by 'double header' teams of straining scrabbling horses, with yells of encouragement and rumbling, scraping sounds from the large wooden wheels and their metal rims as they scrambled up the pot-holed driveway past the church

During the war years many of these low-lying acres had been ploughed up and used for cereal crops – on official instructions. It was not possible to attempt to plough these in a normal spring until mid-March at the earliest, and so nothing was planted other than barley and occasionally oats. The same system applied to the corn crops. Again, ricks were just not possible down in the flood plain, so they too had to be hauled up to the rickyard. The coming of the threshing box brought a frisson of excitement. Its arrival was always preceded by a distant growing rumble until there it was coming up the drive. Drawn by a steam engine, the type used on fairgrounds, the threshing box itself was a massive construction probably eight to nine feet high, five feet wide and twelve to fourteen feet long, with enormous flywheels and pulley wheels.

To get up the steep muddy slope into the rickyard required a considerable amount of skill. First the box was lined up and then the steam engine was uncoupled and driven right up beyond the furthest ricks. Great lugs were dropped down into the earth and a long hawser was taken down to the waiting threshing box. This was then winched up through the mud to the required position between the ricks. We were advised to stand well back while all this took place. There had been quite a few well-publicised occurrences in which the hawser wire had snapped, with fatal results to anybody standing unprotected in the vicinity.

The corn ricks were dismantled systematically, with one person throwing the sheaves on to the top of the machine where an operative crouched, cutting the restraining twine and guiding the loosened sheaf into the inferno of rumbling rollers. To an onlooker the whole process looked extremely dangerous. My usual task was to unpick the meticulous pattern of the corn rick. We had built them carefully the previous autumn by placing row after row around the rick with the ears of corn towards the middle of the rick. The next row in was laid with the butt end level with the centre of the preceding sheaf, and so on until you reached the centre of the rick.

Unpacking was the same operation in reverse. There was a law enforced in those years which stated that, before threshing, wire netting had to be wound around the base of the rick to a height of about four feet. This was to assist in slaying the hordes of rats that had come in from the fields as winter arrived. As the rick was slowly lowered, you were aware of the increasing activity beneath your feet as the inhabitants began to get restive; some of them, when they broke cover, were enormous, as big as feral cats. In the end it was pandemonium, everybody diving in to hit them with anything to hand. I remember that one year a large rick contained 181 rats, not counting the ones that escaped.

I have a remarkably clear memory of one occasion when the old boy to whom I was feeding the sheaves suddenly let out an anguished yell and began to clutch one

27

of his trouser legs in some agitation. The younger fraternity always wore wellingtons, but he was one of the old school and was wearing hobnail boots. A terrorised rodent had tried to escape up his trouser leg, but luckily he was also of the school that had pieces of string known as yorks (or yarks) around their trousers just below the knee. If he hadn't been prepared in this manner the results could well have been extremely painful.

As the corn emerged at the rear of the thresher it was fed into large sacks that when full weighed two hundredweight, or 224lbs. These were then lifted out of the mud onto a higher flat surface, usually an old cart. It was up to the fitter and younger males to carry these fully laden sacks, balanced across their shoulders, to the granary some fifty yards distant.

Often this meant staggering through almost knee-deep mud, which threatened to pull your kneecaps out of their sockets. It was not just one sack, but often twenty or thirty. I can remember being roped in to perform this feat straight after cycling the five miles from school – as I was six foot one even if I was still only fifteen. Some of the onlookers were approaching pensionable age, so they could hardly be blamed for standing back and offering their heartfelt appreciation. Then, of course, it would be off to get the cows in and attend to them for the next two or three hours.

You just accepted that this was how life was. The great contrast to most ordinary jobs was the realisation that no matter what hour it was the cows had to be milked and the other animals fed. It wasn't possible to say 'it's past my time to knock off, I'm going', as animals would die: the cows had to be relieved of their milk, of that there was no question.

*****

One rather more pleasant task on early winter days was sorting and packing vast quantities of the various varieties of apples usually known as 'keepers'. We had twenty-two acres of apple orchard. My father had been a keen apple grower and was connected to the Long Ashton research

station near Bristol. The trees were pruned every year and every tree had a metal nametag attached to one of its lower branches. There were so many varieties, many of them long disappeared from British orchards. First were the summer apples such as Beauty of Bath, Worcester Pearmain and more. We didn't have any Cox's Orange Pippin, but there was a very old half-dead tree that lasted for years – a King of the Pippin, apparently almost the only one left in captivity. Others included Keswicks, Normantons and Lord Hindlips as well as all the cooking varieties, such as Bramley Seedlings, Warner Kings, Warner Seedlings and the like. Much of the autumn was taken up with the picking of these apples. The varieties that didn't keep were sorted and packed in 40lb boxes, lined with newspapers, polished and sent off by the lorryload to Leeds, Sheffield and Manchester.

Straight after the war these apples sold very well and must have been most welcome in those northern cities. Food rationing was still in operation and foreign fruit imports were few and far between. This was in stark contrast to the immediate pre-war years when farming, like much else, was in a dreadful state economically. My father could send lorryloads of scrupulously wrapped and packed apples to Sheffield, often only to receive an invoice charging for the transport. One year it got so bad that he resorted to shaking all the trees. After making the usual 1,000 gallons of cider that he averaged every year, he rolled all the apples into the ground

Down in one corner of the home orchard there were two large trees of russets; they weren't the usual russets but almost unique 'carroway' russets. They were lovely. Other fruit aficionados would take cuttings of these gems to graft onto their own trees. I remember as an eight or nine

year old being encouraged to graft cuttings on rows of newly planted stock. Mine were mainly Laxton Superbs, but sadly all have paid the price of progress in the twentieth century. Apple orchards are now very rare except in the Garden of England: the bit of Kent untouched by motorways, that is.

Chapter Five

Many of those post-war winters were extremely cold, often for a considerable time. Snow lay for weeks and the ground was bone hard. During these periods the cows were kept inside the long low-beamed cowshed permanently. The daily task of cleaning out more than thirty cows and renewing the straw on which they lay was a matter of an hour or more, instead of the twenty minutes usually taken to clean up after morning milking. Great heaps of soiled straw and cow muck arose in the fold yard beyond the wide concrete runway that ran beside the cowshed, loose boxes and pigsties.

Throughout the long cold winter months one of the daily tasks was kale cutting. It ranked with sprout picking as a particularly cold and unpleasant job. Kale was harvested in a style that could easily have been the same as a hundred years before, apart from the fact that growing kale as a cattle food was a comparatively recent phenomenon. A wooden two-wheeled horse-drawn tipping cart was used. These are often visible in ancient photographs of farming in the late nineteenth century – those archetypal snaps of apparently happy crowds of farm workers leaning on their pikes and rakes.

How many people were employed per acre in those days? Still, they were probably paid a mere pittance, and their smiling faces probably denoted that they'd eaten that day for a change and had sampled a little farm cider before the clicking of the shutter.

Kale grew to quite a considerable height and had thick hard stems the size of a human wrist. You cut through these stems using a long-handled billhook. With such an implement it was possible to take a reasonable

swing with well-timed acceleration to the point of impact –
reminiscent of the movement in cricket that is employed in
a hoick over the square leg boundary.

*****

Undertaking odd jobs and helping with various tasks
around the farm was a character I'd known practically all
my life. My father had employed Ted Merchant as a carter
in those pre-tractor years. He was old now and should have
retired: he'd been a drummer boy in the Boer War and had
been on the Western Front fifteen or so years after that. He
had married quite late, probably for security, and quickly
realised that he had acquired a manager. At least she put
some order into his life, I suppose. Even so, the old chap
was obviously happier away from home and was pleasant
enough company. Usually glowing considerably with the
effects of unlimited free cider by mid-morning, he would
accompany me on various jobs, keeping up a nonstop
description of days in the trenches and elsewhere.

His conversation was notorious for being interspersed with colourful expletives.

On this particular day he was leaning against the cart. His most common jest was that he liked to watch folks work while he talked. The fact that he was barely five feet tall probably saved his life that day. Aggravated by a particularly resilient kale stem, I indulged in a particularly aggressive swing and the billhook fled from my wet, freezing, ice-covered hands and embedded its point in the wooden overhang above the wheel of the cart, making a considerable thwacking noise as it quivered just inches above the old chap's head. It was a scene from any early western, the arrival of the first arrow. For once in his life he was speechless, but not for long. There followed the greatest stream of colourful expletives that it has ever been my lot to experience, but they culminated in a great guffaw of mirth. It was the nervous laughter of someone who realised how close a shave he'd just had. He wasn't the only person feeling relieved on that hillside that morning. Even the old farm dog barked enthusiastically.

Ted's late marriage probably prevented him from ending his days in the local workhouse, or 'the Grubber' as it was referred to by all and sundry. The fact that he had served his country in two wars wouldn't have saved him from such an undignified end. It's amazing that as late as the Second World War the poor were packed off like redundant animals to live out their final years in the workhouse. The most despicable aspect of the system was the way that long-married couples were separated, never again to live together as man and wife. So much for 'Victorian values'!

Another Poor Law rule, still in operation in Edwardian times, was that male inmates were made to move constantly between the various 'homes' – in order to impress upon them that they had no right to a permanent place of residence. My mother, born Gladys Phelps, was a farmer's daughter, born in the very last years of the reign of Queen Victoria, and lived at Duckswich Farm, beside the main road between Upton upon Severn and Ledbury. Apparently the able-bodied men had to walk the fourteen miles between Upton and Ledbury, and stay on the

Herefordshire side of the hills for two nights before being 'allowed' to walk back to Upton. This continued *ad infinitum*. My mother remembered how they got to know these unfortunates as they passed back and forth. She would recount how her mother used to supply them with food and cider to help them on their way.

Another recollection about her life as an adolescent at Duckswich Farm gives an insight into life in those far-off days. I asked her whether she remembered seeing her first car. 'Yes I do, clearly,' she exclaimed brightly. 'Old Doctor Nash from Upton was the first person to have a car anywhere around.' Then she sighed and smiled. 'He was the bane of poor Mother's existence. She would see him coming up over Palace Pitch in a great cloud of dust and would dash out to get all her washing in off the clothes-line.'

*****

As the post-war years passed farmers began to acquire more sophisticated tractors, and balloon rubber tyres became the norm. Large International Farmalls, Allis Chalmers, orange Case tractors and bright green John Deeres became quite common. But all my stepfather ever possessed was one of the early wartime standard Fordsons with iron wheels with spade lugs. In cold weather it was the very devil to start. The spade-lugged wheels made it quite a dangerous machine in some situations, especially as it didn't really have brakes. The clutch acted as a transmission brake, but this was merely a thin piece of bent metal that emerged from below the back axle. Driving in wet and muddy wellingtons, it was not unusual to stamp down on the clutch, whereupon your foot would slip forward off the clutch lever and become wedged between it and the axle. Usually there was time to push the throttle forwards, decelerate and extricate the offending muddy boot before anything too dangerous happened. But there were the odd occasions when disaster was only just averted by leaning forward and switching the ignition lever into the off position. Although great clouds of black smoke would sail towards the heavens the old thing would eventually stop.

One incident that more than fifty years on is still imprinted on my memory happened this way. I was ploughing with a three furrow trailing plough, which required almost continuous attention. This meant that I was perpetually leaning back off the tractor seat, steering with one hand and adjusting furrow depth with the other. It was on the same spot as the kale cutting incident, which was quite a steep gradient, with wide bands of wet grey clay running across it at intervals. Passing through these belts of clay made the plough really dig in, which in turn caused the tractor to slow down, sometimes almost to a stop if I didn't quickly alter the depth of the shares. On this occasion I was frantically trying to reset the plough depth, leaning back, when it became obvious that I had to stop the tractor. I heaved myself forward to plant my foot on the clutch, but the usual happened and my foot was caught with the clutch still in its original position. The shares dug in deeper and suddenly the front of the tractor began to rise off the stubble. With great difficulty I managed to reach the ignition lever and switch it off, but by this time the front wheels were three feet off the ground and the fuel tank, normally horizontal, was at an angle of almost forty-five degrees.

I was trapped; I couldn't do anything else. There was a great spluttering and smoke everywhere. The old Fordson seemed to shudder philosophically, then the front fell to earth with a great rattling thud.

I sat there for a while before carrying on. Farming is quite a dangerous occupation. I was probably the only person on the farm that particular day. The nearest human being would have been almost a mile distant. Rubber tyred tractors in such conditions behaved differently. They merely spun their wheels, whereas spade lugs dug in and the engine then began to revolve around the rear wheels, as it were. It would have been a most unpleasant way to end my young life, crushed beneath a twenty ton tractor.

*****

The cold weather that arrived on Boxing Day 1946 lasted for weeks, culminating in early March with the heaviest

snowfall in living memory. The farm was situated on a loop road off a relatively main thoroughfare. Our driveway gate was probably two miles from the main road and for most of its four miles the loop road ran between deep banks.

Coinciding with the snowfall there was a gale force wind. This blizzard caused drifting that had to be seen to be believed. The places where the lane lay between high banks were filled with snow up to eight feet deep, and any depressions on the farmland were similarly flattened out. Everything stopped. We were cut off from the outside world for more than a week, but luckily the phone lines survived. The cows had to be milked, although the milk lorries were unable to collect the churns that usually stood on a high platform by the drive gate. Some milk was fed to the pigs and the rest had to be emptied on to the land – as most of the drains were frozen solid.

At long last a thaw arrived. The snows that had melted higher up the Severn and Teme caused the highest flood of the Severn ever. We were again virtually isolated, and nearby Upton was cut off from the surrounding rural communities. Food was in short supply: there had been no bread since the great snowfall. The bakers and grocers who normally toted their wares around the villages in large

vans clubbed together and organised deliveries in army
DUKW amphibious landing craft, loaned from the nearby
army ordnance depot at Ashchurch, near Tewkesbury. It
was a bit like being relieved after an occupation.

But this was the pre-Beeching era and it was still
possible to get into Upton in an emergency by walking
along the railway embankment. Until the early sixties a
train service still ran between Ashchurch junction and
Great Malvern, through some very picturesque terrain. It
ran four or five times a day, and stopped in Tewkesbury,
Ripple, Upton and Malvern Wells. One of these trains
rattled northwards and stopped at Ripple station at almost
exactly five to one every day. Its progress was clearly
visible from our side of the river, and if you missed the tell-
tale puffs of white smoke among the trees you were always
aware of the toot as it left Ripple station. It was a reliable
reminder that lunchtime was upon us.

The embankment above Upton served as a natural
grandstand along the southern side of the picturesque
cricket ground, which lay opposite the nineteenth-century
New Church with its tall spire and golden stonework.
(There was a much older church tower at the other end of
town, near the river, colloquially referred to as the
Pepperpot because of its squat appearance and domed
tower: the rest of this church had been demolished in
1937 – but the tower still remains today as a prominent
landmark.)

The embankment beside the cricket ground also
served as a temptation when batting from the far end.
Many people over the years had attempted to clear it
completely but the ball always seemed to end up falling
onto the railway track. Sometime around 1949 or 1950 the
first complete clearance was achieved by the legendary Reg
Perks (Worcestershire and England) while playing in a
benefit match. Many years later another complete carry
was achieved, but modesty prevents me from disclosing the
player's identity.

Some years later the whole embankment was
removed, and the main road beyond was re-routed over
what had always been a landmark in the area – a large, low
burial ground affectionately known as Tom Tiddler's Island,

— ROSES / THE SEVERN AT UPTON —

which lay in a field at the bottom of Tunnel Hill. When the Severn was in flood this mound became a virtual island, hence its name. Its significance lay in the fact that it was the final resting place of the many local victims of the Great Plague. To build a road over that mound has always seemed to me to denote a lack of respect, or perhaps it was just a thoughtless disregard for history.

These reminiscences of the Great 1947 Flood

remind me of a winter some years before when the floodwater that covered the whole low-lying Severn Valley froze solid. Then the water receded, leaving great sheets of thick ice suspended above the fields, attached to the hedges and small trees. My brother and I managed to get through a hole in the ice and we walked around underneath the canopy. My mother was not at all pleased to hear where we had been, I remember. Not that it was all that dangerous a thing to do, but it was very muddy down there.

When the ice thawed that winter it came down between the main banks of the Severn in a great crashing tide of breaking sheets of ice, making a loud ringing, almost metallic, sound. I don't think it has happened again since that particular winter. I remember thinking that this must be similar to the thaw in Canada.

Chapter Six

The summer of 1947 was paradoxically one of the longest and hottest ever. This coincided with a change in the method used to collect the heavy crops of hay from the meadows that lay beside the Severn. In previous years the grass had been cut, usually in the early morning when it was covered in dew, left to dry, then turned – in bygone days by hordes of workers by hand, and later with a horse-drawn implement known as a swathe turner.

The swathe turner was converted, merely by attaching extra tines to the centre sections, into a device that created lines or 'walleys' of dried hay about ten feet apart, which then awaited horse-drawn wagons. Attached to the rear of these wagons was an implement called a hay loader, which obviated the need for gangs of people to hand up forkfuls of hay to the person on the wagon building the load.

The finished load was hauled up out of the flood plain to the rickyard behind the cowshed, where a large hayrick was built. The hay was transferred from wagon to rick with a rather sophisticated apparatus. Attached to a tall pole, probably forty feet high, was a horizontal pole about twelve feet long. On the end of this secondary pole dangled a large metal four-pronged claw. With the aid of a pony at ground level, whose harness was connected to a long hawser that moved through a system of pulleys and wheels, the claw was thrust into the hay on the wagon. This was then swung up and over to the rick. A cord was pulled and the hay was deposited from the open claw. This method of rick building must have been used for only about twenty years. It was remarkably efficient, but progress was at hand.

Our new method of hay collection used a hay sweep with long tines which was attached to the front of a tractor. The hay was swept up to either a stationary baler or made into a temporary rick that then awaited the arrival of the baling contractor.

This was the hardest work of the whole year on the farm. The hay that had been swept up to the baler was bound up tightly and required brute force to disentangle it with a pitchfork (always known as a 'pike'). The hay was then lifted by hand the seven or eight feet onto the large wooden chute mounted on top of the stationary bailer. We

did not, unfortunately, possess a box elevator, which would have made things so much easier. But this didn't seem to worry my stepfather as he circled the field collecting the hay with his tractor and sweep, puffing away on his pipe. Next the hay was rammed into a horizontal baling chamber and metal double needles were inserted at intervals. Baling wire was threaded through the needles and tied manually by a person working on the other side. The bales that emerged from these early machines were about four feet long and thirty inches square, and often weighed over 200lbs. They were like great lead ingots.

There were no easy jobs. The wire operators were

working in a great cloud of dust and hayseeds. The wires were far from pliable and their hands were frequently covered in blood. Added to this there was always the element of danger posed by sharp wire being pushed through at face level. Even so, the worst part was handling the bales as they shot out of the end of the baling chamber. They were stacked up to ten high, so the stacker had to carry bales on his back up steps as the rick grew, leaping back down in time to catch the next bale before it fell to the ground. As the rick's height increased a large plank was placed on the end of the chamber, so the bales could be shunted up to the higher level. This was all very well, but the bales seemed to become heavier and heavier the higher the plank was raised.

In those days nobody ever worked at these tasks without shirts, probably because there was so much dust and hayseeds. The sharp ends of the wires from the bales ripped the back of your shirt, so by nightfall your back was a mess of sweat, blood and hayseeds.

Down in those low-lying river meadows with their high hedges the heat was often almost unbearable, and the lack of any breeze ensured an atmosphere that was oppressive in the extreme. Whenever there was a brief stop we dashed to the nearest bit of shade. Nobody wanted to spend any more time than necessary in the full glare of the sun. It was quite a shock in later years to meet people who thought the ultimate joy in life was lying for hours in the burning rays of the sun. Incomprehensible.

At about six o'clock someone would have to be off to get the cows in and prepare for the evening milking. Everyone else carried on baling for a while before trudging back up the farm for a quick cup of tea; then on with the never-ending farm chores. For weeks in the summer months, if the weather was good enough, it was quite common to work for sixteen hours every day.

I have memories of proceedings being curtailed by sudden thunderstorms and of standing in the middle of a field to let the rain soak me completely, washing the hayseeds and dust away. Then you did take your shirt off! Thunderstorms are more dangerous if you stand under a tree.

*****

Once a year a particularly brutal ritual was played out. Why it had to be so barbarous escaped me, even then. On most farms in that era a chosen pig was retained for the farmer and his family. Just as food rationing continued long after the war had ended, so did this practice. In those days most communities seemed to boast a pig killer, an itinerant person usually of necessarily insensitive disposition, who would roll up and perform the deed. The man who used to attend at my stepfather's behest would probably have applied for Albert Pierrepoint's job with glee had it become vacant, especially if he could have used an axe and not a rope.

He had a theory that using the stipulated humane killing pistol had an adverse effect on the subsequent flavour of the meat, so he cut the terrified animal's throat with a large and incredibly sharp knife. I realise there are still religions that stipulate animals should be slaughtered in this manner. That just adds to my overall disgust for the act, and diminishes even further my lack of respect for any form of religion.

Being the biggest and strongest person around, I usually had to hang onto the front end of the pig, with my arms around its front legs or even its neck. I can only compare the terrified screams of the pig to that of the rolling mill at the Steel Company of Wales at Port Talbot when that was in operation. The noise was ear piercing. From just a few inches away it was appalling. Shouts of ''ang on 'im, Geoffrey . . .' and 'oh bugger it, I've dropped me knife . . .', all delivered through a haze of alcoholic fumes, made the whole affair difficult to take.

The last time I was involved this despicable sadist

made at least two inaccurate attempts to kill the pig, before being so successful that I was soaked by a great surge of warm blood that covered the top half of my body and matted my hair. I can remember deciding there and then that I would never again take part in such an act. It was a decision to which I've kept. The cruelty shown by some, but certainly not all, of the farming community, I have always found difficult to understand. You have only to watch the way some people load cattle into a cattle lorry to see this. They yell and flay the beasts with long ash sticks, hitting them at least ten times more than is necessary. Perhaps it's just human nature. The urge that makes people want to join the marines, or paratroopers, or any of those military outfits which encourage the belief that you're not a real soldier until you've killed another human being in battle.

*****

Looking back to the life we led all those years ago, it's easy to forget just how lonely it was, especially when compared with today's existence and all the electronic gadgetry, personal transport, mobile phones and so much more that we take entirely for granted. Often we would work all day and not see, or converse with, another human being. There were not even tractor radios. It might well have been beneficial for our self-sufficiency, but it did have its disadvantages.

In winter, overcome by weariness when the cows were eventually tucked up for the night, we retreated indoors for food and rest. It was often very tempting to relax and read or listen to the wireless until the early hours. In my teens I must have read hundreds of books. I remember keeping a list, but heaven knows where it is now. I wish I still had it

The nearest town was almost four miles distant. There was no television, of course, and the delights of cycling had long since disappeared. After all those years of pedalling ten miles every day in the pursuit of education, I felt I had been inoculated against any desire to cycle anywhere ever again. But of course I did. It was necessary to be part of society and so I rode the potholed lanes to the

45

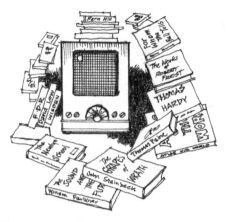

pubs of Upton upon Severn and to the Sabrina cinema at the more distant Tewkesbury. These trips were usually made with a degree of reluctance, and almost always alone. Although I spent most days at the wheel of a tractor and drove my stepfather's ex-US army Willys Jeep about the farm at all times, there was no way I could consider running a vehicle of my own.

Each year merged into the next. Looking back on it, the numbing boredom of drudgery seven days a week had the effect of eliminating all else from the mind. That's probably not totally accurate because those of us who were interested were kept informed about the outside world by the wireless. There was also sport to sustain those who weren't totally consumed by agriculture.

Despite all the hard work, there was always the realisation that I was surrounded by an abundance of natural splendour. Just to take one example: on an early winter's evening you were sometimes confronted by the magnificence of towering leafless elm trees and the breathtaking beauty of a full moon behind this infinite tracery. There was usually the distraction of multitudes of rooks and their cacophony, but that was a price worth paying.

The usual effect of such ethereal dreaming was catching your mud-laden wellingtons in submerged barbed wire and falling headlong into the oozing mire.

Chapter Seven

continued to play cricket whenever it was possible. Village cricket predominated in my life in these years, as playing more demanding club cricket required a greater degree of dedication and practice than farming allowed. Even so, I did play in occasional benefit games against some of my heroes, people like Reg Perks, Dick Howorth, Bob Wyatt, Peter Jackson, the young Henry Horton and even the inimitable Roly Jenkins.

Village cricket until the early fifties was usually played on farmers' fields, on a mown square that spent the week protected behind a removable fence – which avoided bovine hoof prints on a 'good length'. In summer the rest of the field was either mowing grass or 'aftermath'. When Saturday arrived the fence around the square was removed, and the game was often played on a large rectangle of mown grass surrounded by a grass wall rising to a height of ten to twelve inches. The only boundaries possible were of the lofted variety for six. A ball hit with maximum power along the ground parted the tall stems for a short way, looking exactly like an escaping rabbit in a cornfield at harvest time.

In the summer of 1947 I remember playing a game against Hasfield on a field not unlike our own river meadows. It was down beyond Haw Bridge, notorious as the location of a headless torso murder hunt that inflamed public excitement in the immediate pre-war years. That same day England scored fifty-two all out at the Oval. It began to look as if I was going to better their score 'off my own bat' as it were, but I eventually succumbed for forty-eight. The amazing thing about that innings is that there were no boundaries at all in my score because of the long grass in the outfield: just singles and twos, not even a three. It must be forty years since any cricket at all was played on that field: so many villages gave up the unequal struggle.

Another vivid memory is of a game at Eldersfield, not so many miles from Hasfield. In a typically rural Gloucestershire setting, the pitch lay across the lane from the village pub, the Butcher's Block as it was known in those days. Apparently the landlord had made it known that if anybody ever hit a six that landed on the small lawn outside the pub, the prize would be a hogshead of beer. I opened our innings with our local policeman, a tall, muscular Irishman, who'd played professional football in his time. He was left-handed and had a penchant for heaving deliveries with great power to the square leg boundary and beyond. It was a hot day, the outfield was particularly long and we were soon hitting out quite freely. The field itself was probably about eight or ten acres in extent and the cricketing area was in one corner. During the course of the afternoon a herd of grazing Friesians, originally at the far end of the field, began to gradually drift nearer.

Obviously they were now within the boundary. Perhaps with a mischievous view to moving these animals, my batting partner essayed a steepling hit toward the encroaching beasts. To everyone's amazement a human figure was suddenly seen among the cows. He calmly caught the ball, claiming the catch! My policeman friend was incandescent. 'I thought you'd come to get the bloody cows in!' he roared, and flung his willow to the ground; but he had to go.

This game was also notable because almost the entire opposing team was arrayed in clothes that probably originated in the nineteenth century. They wore heavy serge grey/black trousers 'half mast' above whitewashed hobnail boots, with braces to keep their trousers up and thick belts just to be sure. Those that didn't wear ties favoured collarless shirts. Most wore dark flat caps and one or two sported droopy moustaches. This was 1947. It's stayed in my memory to this day.

Later I put a ball onto the lawn at about the fifth attempt, so the evening passed happily. The policeman had gone.

I never played there again, and sometimes wonder if things ever changed. The pub is certainly still there.

*****

In the winter I chased a soccer ball over the fields of Worcestershire with a certain amount of success. Even if I had been good enough to climb the ladder, and I wasn't really, there wasn't the financial incentive to professional sport that there is now. I knew people who turned down the chance of fame at football and cricket, purely on the grounds of insufficient monetary reward.

Just after hostilities finished I had scored four goals in a 'victory' cup final, the final of a serious competition involving mature players, including many servicemen. My goals included a right-footed corner kick from the right-wing corner flag that swung at the last minute and sailed in just under the crossbar, still rising. Technically it was, of course, a bad corner, but it felt good at the time. After this performance there were rumours, but nothing ever happened. At the end of the game the other members of our victorious eleven attempted to 'chair' me off the field in celebration. I took to my heels and outran them back to the changing room. I can remember thinking 'I expect there will be other times' . . . but there never were in the more than five hundred games of competitive football I was to play in the years thereafter.

That had been on a Saturday afternoon before Christmas 1945. On the Monday morning, as we stood around in the kitchen after morning milking, the local postman arrived. He launched into a very flattering description of my triumphant moments which he had observed at first hand, it appeared. It was the first time my family had heard of it. The old postman was waxing lyrical, prophesying a glowing future,when my stepfather brusquely moved towards the door, saying, 'Well come on, Geoffrey, you'd better get on and feed the calves. We can't stand around talking all day, there's work to be done.' There was no mention at all of the football after that.I can well imagine a similar occurrence nowadays: proud grandparents would dash out and purchase expensive boots, and more. It's another world. No, those years were primarily seven days a week slavery.

Among all the memories of local football one match stands out: not the game itself, as I can't even remember if we won, but the venue. I think it was a semi-final of the Hereford Hospital Cup, played in late March at a village called Rushall between Ledbury and Ross-on-Wye. At that time, before insecticides became rampant, there was an area around Dymock, probably about eight square miles, that was almost unique. In spring the fields were completely covered with wild daffodils; not the tall, waving variety, but a shorter plant with small flowers. People would journey for miles to observe them and were not averse to taking armfuls home. Before 1914 this was the area beloved by the so-called Dymock poets, who all lived in the area – Lascelles Abercrombie, Edward Thomas, John Drinkwater and the legendary American New England laureate Robert Frost.

ROBERT FROST

" One could do worse
Than be a swinger
of birches "

What they made of the daffodils I do not know. As we trooped out onto the football pitch that day the scene before us amazed me. We were to play on a sea of yellow daffodils. Right to the hedges it was all daffodils. I must have been playing right back, and every long clearance up field resulted in a great shower of yellow petals. I didn't enjoy it too much; it seemed like sacrilege.

*****

Village cricket and local soccer were to me what 'country sports' were all about. I've had a lifelong aversion to blood sports of all descriptions. Killing living beings for sport has always seemed to me to be depravity defined. I was not alone in my abhorrence of hunting. There were plenty among the farming community to whom it was anathema. Quite apart from the degrading ethics of the whole thing hunting was such a nuisance – fences were broken down, gates were left open and it made such a mess of our crops. To many people the huntsmen were definitely not welcome. It was a relic of ages past, of tenant farmers tugging their forelocks as the squire rode by. Then there were the people who'd moved into the country from town, eager, hearty young males who would appear with shining twelve bores in the crook of their tweedy hacking jackets. 'I say, would you mind if I took me gun round the farm shootin'?' they would enquire.

I tried not to be rude, but my usual response was, 'I'd rather you didn't. I quite enjoy seeing hares and pheasants about the place. They look infinitely better alive than dead.' Incredulity was the usual response.

The only living thing that I ever shot was a rabbit. It horrified me. We had a .22 rifle and would amuse ourselves shooting at tins against brick walls, and practising sinking tin cans bobbing on the local brook. One day I was walking around the farm and saw a rabbit about 120 yards away. Why I decided to fire at it I'll never know. A shiny, healthy animal eating away, occasionally giving a little hop as it moved to tastier pasture. A vision of that sort gladdens the heart of someone who truly loves nature. But for some unknown reason I raised the rifle and fired. I hit it but didn't kill it. The animal let out a high-pitched scream just like a baby in excruciating pain. I flung down the gun and ran uphill to the stricken rabbit. Its innards were exposed on the grass. I quickly dispatched the unfortunate beast in the time-honoured way, with the side of my hand to the back of its neck. It mercifully stopped screaming. I was appalled by what I'd done and vowed never to do such a thing again. How anybody could possibly derive any pleasure from killing anything as beautiful as a hare astounds me.

Like anybody connected with farming I've seen the damage and the carnage that foxes can do. The answer, surely, is to shoot them, if possible at the scene of the crime. The idea of making a social occasion, a piece of pageantry, out of the whole thing has always appalled me. How can it be described as a sport? To start with, an 'earth stopper' is dispatched before the meet takes place. This ensures that any fox clever enough to avoid the buffoons huffing and puffing in his wake finds his lair barred, and is left to be torn apart. If the fox does go to ground he is dug up and thrown to the baying hounds, who are momentarily delayed so as to give the victim a few seconds' start. Perhaps most despicable of all is the distasteful custom of smearing the faces of children with blood as a sort of indoctrination.

I've seen plenty of examples of the cruelty exhibited by foxes, but that doesn't make it any less degrading to pursue them as a sport, deriving pleasure from their suffering. Not that foxes necessarily kill just for food. Etched into my memory is the scene that was revealed to me in my youth, on opening the door of a fowls' house that had been placed on some stubble, so the hens could glean the bits of corn left by harvesting. I'd been round the previous evening to check the birds were safely locked inside, with all entrances closed. Opening the door the following morning, I was confronted by a scene of complete mayhem. There were feathers and dead carcasses everywhere. We afterwards counted 112 dead fowls, practically all of them missing their legs.

Apparently Reynard had managed somehow to wriggle between the slatted floor and the removable wooden floor eight inches below. While there he had systematically chewed off every leg of the hens above, probably lying on his back. Because the henhouse was in a distant field nobody had heard the terrified squawking. It was a dreadful sight, but it was nature in the raw.

I had an uncle who farmed 500 acres below the Cotswold escarpment. He eventually banned the local hunt from his land, purely on ethical grounds. He was an exceptional man, unusual among the agricultural community in his attitude to life. So many farmers are brutalised by their calling, but he was not so affected. Usually when a dairy cow's productive life ends it is quickly dispatched to the abattoir or knacker's yard. My uncle had a field that he reserved for these dowagers of the dairy, a kind of retirement home. Sometimes they lived for quite a long time. They were obviously a financial liability, but he was happy to lean on the gate, talking to his beloved sheepdog and watching his animals enjoying their deserved retirement.

Chapter Eight

rom late 1945 until the summer of 1949 the idea of taking a holiday was never mentioned. The occasional day (or rather half day, as there was always morning milking and so on), was grudgingly allowed. These rare jaunts entailed a three-mile cycle ride to Upton upon Severn and then a bus ride the twelve miles to Worcester, but they were like gold dust. For example, I remember seeing the Australians open their cricket tour at Worcester in 1948. In 1930, 1934 and 1938 Don Bradman had scored over 200 at Worcester as a matter of habit. Everybody at New Road that day expected the great man to help himself to another double century. It's all so clear in my memory. He calmly went to his century, then spooned the ball high into the air above the square, put his bat under his arm, nodded to the bowler, to Arthur Morris at the other end and strode off to the pavilion. I can remember feeling quite disappointed. Still, I had actually seen in the flesh the greatest batsman the world had ever known.

In 1947 Gloucestershire and Middlesex met at the Cheltenham cricket festival. It was a famous occasion, as both counties were in a position to win the championship. On the opening day, a Saturday, twenty-one wickets fell. It became known as 'the day of Cliff Monk's catch', a truly wonderful boundary catch taken after a desperate skelter culminating in a spectacular dive.

Years after this occasion it would appear that everybody in Gloucestershire was there that day, and yet I don't recall such a vast audience. Perhaps that's being unduly cynical.

I also saw the legendary Charlie Barnett (who once scored ninety-nine before lunch in a test match against Australia) score 223 in a day at the old Wagon Works ground in Gloucester.

Other memorable sporting memories included seeing Cottage Rake win the first of his three Gold Cups at Cheltenham's Prestbury Park at long odds. This was Vincent O'Brien's first big race success outside Ireland. Little did anyone realise then that he would become such an icon in the racing world. There was no luxury grandstand viewing in those days for people in our position. If I recall it was four shillings and six pence to stand with the rest of the proletariat in the scruffy old 'cabbage patch' as it was known, but it felt like a seat in history at the time.

In the late summer of 1949 I went on my first holiday since our customary week at Weston-super-Mare before the war. (If proof were needed of how attached we were as children to our lives on the family farm, something must be gauged from the fact that I can remember spending most of the week at Weston, however nice the weather, the donkey rides and so on, counting the hours to when we'd return to the space and freedom of home.) My brother and I eventually coaxed his 1937 Hillman Minx all the way down the A38 to Torquay. To be honest I don't really remember much about that week. Most of it seemed to be spent in licensed premises. That stale beer smell of a pub at opening time returns to my nostrils. I think we went to see Ted Heath and his band, and I have a very clear recollection of witnessing the arrival in Torbay of the Smith brothers in their rowing boat, having been the first people to have rowed across the Atlantic, or at least since Eric the Red, whenever he did it.

Chapter Nine

By the spring of 1951 I had had enough of the endless drudgery. Three pounds a week and my keep wasn't getting me anywhere. I was never remotely involved in the running or planning of anything that happened on the farm. So I managed to buy an old secondhand Fordson Major tractor, got hold of a few basic implements and began to work as a contractor. I was entering the stressful world of the self-employed. Later I bought a secondhand engine-mounted pick-up baler. This was an American import, quite a bit larger than the trailer-type baler that became popular later. It was an International B50 complete with a high revving two litre Wisconsin petrol engine perched high up, presumably out of the dust generated by the baling. After spending that summer baling hay in surrounding villages I was beginning to worry about what would last me through the winter. Obviously there would be some work to be done, baling hayricks, but would it be enough? Would I get enough ploughing? I was used to working almost 365 days a year. Early in September a friend, who had some land in East Anglia as well as by the Severn, contacted me and suggested that it might be worth transporting my tractor and pick-up bailer to Essex to bale straw that autumn. He even offered to lend me his seven ton Maudslay lorry to transport it there.

Within a week I was on my way east. There was a bit of a worrying moment driving up Fish Hill onto the Cotswolds, when both bits of machinery seemed to shift a little within the carefully tied restraining ropes. Part of the baler protruded beyond the edge of the lorry bed into the passing traffic and required the statutory piece of red cloth. A quick inspection reassured me that all was well, and late that evening I pulled up in his farm at Dedham, in the valley of the Stour. This was Constable country: Flatford Mill was just down the road.

I then caught the train to London and returned to Worcestershire, to collect my old faithful ex-GPO Morris series E van, throw some clothes in together with an old mattress and blankets, and set off again to East Anglia.

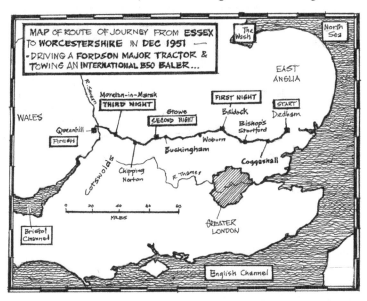

For the next six or eight weeks I worked practically all the hours that daylight allowed, before falling into the back of the old Morris and going to sleep. I didn't even bother to eat much, certainly not regularly. If I was passing a roadside café between farms I would stop for a quick fry-up, tea and away. Once, when the weather broke for a few days, I went berserk and booked into a local pub for a proper night's rest and a bath. Luxury indeed.

People were very kind. I think some of them took pity on me, and invited me in to eat with them.

There were one or two mishaps, but not too many. Once I broke one of the springs on the knotting mechanism. Removing the offending bit of metal I foolishly attempted to alter the shape of it by placing it in a vice that I had in the van. As I tried to bend it into the position that I had envisaged, the spring shot out of the vice and hit me in the eye. Luckily it was sideways on at the moment of impact, but for about an hour I couldn't see a thing. I was miles away from anywhere at the end of a long flat East Anglian farm lane. Luckily the farmer arrived eventually, to see how the baling was progressing. I think he was quite shocked by what had happened, and I was taken off in his Ford Pilot to his farmhouse and plied with hot tea and aspirins. I suppose I should have gone to Colchester accident and emergency, but I didn't. For a few days things were a bit misty in that one eye, but I was back at work baling and had other things to worry about.

The winds blew quite strongly off the North Sea in that area and by early November it was quite cold and wintry. For about ten more days I baled straw from ricks – but that seemed to be about that and I began to think about returning home.

In the intervening weeks my friend had sold the lorry. He had two cattle lorries, which I'd occasionally driven, but the baler was too wide for them. I approached British Road Services and they quoted me something over £150 to take the two implements back to Worcestershire. That was a lot of money in those days. In the end I decided I'd drive it back, all 160 miles of it. TYO, paraffin that is, was pretty cheap and my time was my own, I reasoned. So I left the machinery there and returned home. If I recall correctly I avoided the rail journey on this occasion by driving one of my friend's cattle boxes back to his farm near Worcester. It was quite a contraption. An articulated lorry, the tractor portion was an ex-American Army GMC, left-hand drive, with twelve forward gears. That is, it had a six-speed gearbox with a reduction box, which had the effect of making six lower gears available in an emergency. With eighteen steers on board it was quite a handful, but I'd driven it before and it seemed too good an opportunity to miss.

A nasty surprise awaited me on my return home. I'd been looking forward to at least a day or two of peace before going back for the machinery, but an official letter informed me that I was to attend the local recruiting offices within a few days and sign on for National Service. I was twenty-two years old, and had been deferred for four and a half years as I was working in agriculture. What they thought I was doing in East Anglia I don't know, but the law's the law. Obviously there was no reason why I should have suddenly been deemed to be no longer eligible for agricultural deferment. I had, if it were possible, been working even harder in a completely agricultural environment. I always had my suspicions that someone, somewhere, had put the boot in and had made an unfounded complaint for their own reason. When I objected I was told to apply to attend a tribunal. It was a difficult situation. I'd always felt it unfair that farmers' sons should be deferred when all our schoolfriends had had to endure the boredom and pointlessness of military life for two long years. Most of my friends had hated it, just the endless boredom of it all, apart from the danger of being dispatched to fight in some unwarranted conflict. But at this stage in my life it was even more difficult to take.

In the First World War farmers' sons were often the first to go. In many cases they joined the local yeomanry and took their own horses with them. My father didn't do that, but he was soon in uniform. He joined the Machine Gun Corps. They rode ancient flat petrol-tanked motorcycles with cow horn handlebars and flatbed sidecars on which a man rode firing a machine gun. I've read that they snorted off towards the enemy lines firing away. Every trip must have been virtually suicidal, but he managed to survive almost four years on the Western Front before transferring to join Allenby's Army in the Levant. My father never said directly what it was like, at least not to our tender ears, but I did once overhear him say to a neighbouring farmer, who'd been there too, that he thought the worst thing about those years of trench warfare was walking on the duckboards through the mud, and the way that eyeless corpses rose out of the mire beside you as you did so.

I think the experience affected him greatly. I can recall him exuding tiny fragments of shrapnel occasionally even after more than twenty years. No one talked about it much. I've often thought about the horrors they must have endured, almost like living in a depiction of hell, like a Hieronymus Bosch painting. No one knew how long it would last. They must have accepted that one day would be your last and then you'd be one of those eyeless corpses. Some idiots maintain that war is noble and glorious. I'm always speechless with anger when listening to such sentiments.

After demobilisation in 1919, my father had opted to return to the Middle East and became an inspector of agriculture in what was then the Anglo-Egyptian Sudan. Before the outbreak of hostilities in 1914 he'd studied at and graduated from the Harper Adams Agricultural College in Shropshire. For the next ten years or so he lived the life of a colonial administrator, supervising the setting up of a new cotton-growing industry on the Gezira Plain, the area between the White and Blue Nile rivers north of Khartoum. I imagine that this was quite a demanding job and the climate was unbelievably hard. In 1924 my parents were married, and both somehow existed in the heat and the sand. My mother used to laugh and recall, 'There wasn't another European woman for 200 miles.' By 1930 I think they had had enough. I imagine those years on the Western Front had taken their toll in many ways.

They returned to England and my father took over the tenancy of Church Farm, Queenhill. Two years later, in the depths of the Depression, the Pull Court estate was dismantled. Many such estates were broken up at this time. The neighbouring farms that made up the Ham Court estate were disposed of, and the large mansion at its centre was unceremoniously demolished. At the Pull Court estate sale my father was able to purchase the farm for £3,000. They were very difficult days for the farming community and I have the feeling that he was only saved by his Sudanese government pension, which helped to supplement his income.

I had an uncle, my mother's eldest brother, who was one of those slaughtered in the appalling stupidity of the First World War. He was a farmer's son and, like so many in those early years of the last century, thought that emigration would be the way to the promised land. So, aged barely twenty, he had sailed to the Antipodes and eventually found work on an outback farm. Then war was declared and within a year he was one of the thousands slaughtered on the beaches of Gallipoli. They didn't stand a chance: victims of an infamous tactical error dreamt up by some blue blood seeking historical glory. One of his close friends, an Australian and one of the few to survive, took it upon himself to come to England after the war to visit my grandparents and hand over various treasured belongings. He eventually married my mother's older sister and they settled in Victoria, never to return. That was before mobile phones and affordable air fares. Apparently in later years he divulged that my uncle Harry had been impaled on the Turkish barbed wire defences for hours, before eventually succumbing. My grandmother was never told, but when I heard about it this added to my rejection of militarism.

Chapter Ten

efore National Service, there was still the business of getting my machinery back home. By some means, it's so long ago I can't remember how, my Morris van was already back at base. So once more I did the lorry driving thing and ended up in Constable country.

Filling the faithful old Fordson Major with TVO, I hitched up the baler and headed westward from Dedham. As the top speed of a Fordson Major was four miles per hour, progress was not exactly breathtaking. It was further compromised by the machinery attached to the tow bar. Not only did it extend about twelve feet backwards, it was so wide that the auger housing protruded into the road further than the central white line.

About every hundred yards I would have to pull into the grass verge and let past the long line of traffic that had built up. Most people waved and parped their horns, but there were always the self-important ones who yelled and pointed accusing fingers. Yes, they were around in those days too.

It was December and I had no lights, so by half past three I had to start looking around for somewhere to stop and park overnight

Just outside Baldock I pulled into a transport café yard and parked among the lorries. There was at least food to eat and a dirty old room in which to read a newspaper. Televisions were quite a rarity in 1951 and there certainly

wasn't one in that establishment. As I had to make use of the available daylight I decided to retire to bed early. The sleeping quarters were even less appealing: about twenty mattresses on old metal bedsteads, all jumbled into an uninviting dormitory. I remember sleeping in my clothes, as it appeared to be the accepted custom. My battered attaché case I tied to the springs underneath the bed, and most particularly I slept on my wallet.

Next day I set off up the A1 towards Biggleswade, and then left to Amptill past the long wall that surrounded Woburn Abbey, through Fenny Stratford, over the A1 and to the old town of Buckingham, past the prison and out the other side. It was getting dark by now and I was approaching a large and rather prestigious hotel standing back from the road behind a sweeping gravel forecourt. Almost without considering my actions I turned off, whirling across the gravel and stopping a little to one side of the majestic steps. As I strode up towards this imposing entrance a man, obviously the manager, appeared between the pillars. 'Can I help?' he enquired, with a friendly smile. 'I hope so,' I replied, and told him of my cross-country expedition and my previous night's experience, and expressed a desire to try a little luxury instead. I must have been quite disreputable by now, but my luck was in. He seemed impressed by the whole idea. 'Fine,' he said. 'Can you take it round the back, and when you come in I'll show you to your room. Room 16, it'll be. Have a bath and a rest and perhaps you'll be down to sample some dinner with us.'

In retrospect the whole journey seems hilarious. It didn't feel like that at the time, believe me, so I felt very grateful to that friendly man. He could so easily have ordered me to leave, but instead he displayed a true humanity. I wish I had written to him in the days that followed, but sadly I didn't.

Clean and refreshed after a good night's sleep, I breakfasted and collected the entourage from the rear of the building. As I chuffed round past the front of the hotel, the manager, some of the other guests and even some of his staff in their pristine white apparel were arrayed on the steps, waving and calling 'bon voyage'. Little scenes like that live in the memory.

On I went through Croughton and the neatness of Aynho, down and over the bridge spanning two railway tracks and the Grand Union canal, and on towards Deddington. I began to feel that I was past the halfway mark. I'd driven this way with cattle lorries, and the bends became progressively more familiar. It was a Saturday morning, and people all over the land were preparing for a break from the pressures of earning a living. Thoughts were turning towards sport, or an evening of jollity. Up here on the high North Oxfordshire Plain, though, the weather was taking a turn for the worse. The sun, so pleasurable on the previous day, had yet to put in an appearance. Over Banbury the skies became darker, assuming a pallor tinged with sepia that was reminiscent of pig manure. A wind arose and the temperature dropped. The mark one Fordson Major was unusually tall and the driver sat 'high in the saddle', as the men of the early west would have it. There was very little protection from the elements, for this was years before anybody thought of such things as cabs on tractors. No heaters, no radio, just the bark of the vertical exhaust a couple of feet ahead. I was unprepared for these conditions. A pair of thin trousers, an open-necked shirt, a sleeveless pullover, an old lightweight summer jacket and a thin belted mackintosh were all that protected me in my lofty seat.

Beyond Deddington it began to snow, almost horizontally. I suppose it was a blizzard. I couldn't remember ever feeling so cold. Winters of farm work had often thrown some pretty icy conditions my way, but there were usually places to shelter and regain your circulation with vigorous arm movements. In those far off years people who worked on the land often draped heavy corn sacks around their shoulders, tied at the front with baler twine. Sometimes another sack would be arranged like a cowl on top of the head, with the rest of it falling away down the back; anything to keep relatively warm and less wet.

Eventually, at about two o'clock, I began the long decline into Chipping Norton with its wide-open market square in front of the market hall. I reined my vehicles up, parked on a convenient space and set off on wobbly legs to find a café. When I eventually found an eating place it was

66

completely empty. I chose a table and sat down. My thighs were tight up against the underside of the metal table, and I was shaking so violently with the cold that everything on the table began to jump up and down and jingle noisily. Even now I can hear that cacophony.

An hour later, with circulation partly restored, I drove off down the hill out of Chipping Norton, past the ancient woollen mill to the left with its massive dark chimneys. I was beginning to feel a trifle weary of the whole escapade. I could head for Stow-on- the-Wold, and then to Tewkesbury, but it would entail another overnight stop. Alternatively . . . at the junction off to the left to Edward Thomas's Adlestrop, I made an instant decision to head on towards Moreton-in-Marsh. The snow had mercifully stopped, but the sky was beginning to darken with the onset of night. Chuffing up to the crossroads in the middle of Moreton, I turned northwards up the Fosse and made a beeline for the railway station that still lies at the far end of the town. Driving into the car park, I grabbed my battered case and headed towards the warmly lit buildings by the platform. Explaining the situation to an enquiring stationmaster, I waited for the next train from London to Shrub Hill Worcester.

On arrival in Worcester I caught a Midland Red bus to Upton, where I adjourned to a local hostelry. Luckily a cricketing acquaintance gave me a lift home in his van. Next day I retraced my steps to Moreton and brought the equipage home. The trek had ended. The big question now was what to do with the tractor and baler. It was midwinter, and nobody wanted either machine at other than a knockdown price. I couldn't keep it, as I had to be trained in the technique of slaughtering other human beings, so I eventually sold it for about a quarter of its purchase price – which made a complete nonsense of all my efforts in East Anglia. I might just as well not have bothered. On top of everything else I was two stone lighter than I had been eight weeks before and my ribs protruded. I tried not to be bitter, but it wasn't easy.

Chapter Eleven

arly in the New Year I had to attend a tribunal in Birmingham. It was almost seven years since I had left formal education, so I'd forgotten what the pompous exercise of power was like. I was more or less marched into a large empty room, and up towards a raised platform at the far end. On this platform, obviously placed there to make a person standing on the lower level feel suitably cowed, sat three quite elderly men. I can remember how small they were: the fact that I was well over six feet tall probably added to their very apparent hostility. The central figure was probably sixty years of age and bristled with self-importance. He had a large military moustache and the acidic countenance of an old time evangelist.

Before I had time to speak he barked out a command: 'stand up straight and keep your hands down to your sides!' I was standing dead upright, but he obviously wanted to humiliate me. I made quite a lucid case for myself, but it was useless in the face of such bigotry. I doubt if he listened to one word of what I had to say.

Some weeks later I received the expected result by post. I was to report in due course to Norton Barracks near Worcester to join the local infantry regiment. Actually, it was almost nine months later that I donned a uniform. During that time all I could do was return to working for my stepfather, with the usual seven days a week toil. It never occurred to me to claim benefit! By the time I arrived at Norton Barracks I was past my twenty-third birthday. To say I was the most unwilling conscript ever could be a slight overstatement, although not by much. But I was sufficiently cunning to play it my way. It was all such an eye opener. I had expected it to be bad, even unpleasant, but this was like attending school for the first day, with vicious teachers.

I had always been interested in current affairs, political history, everything that was going on in the world, but the degree of ignorance in that place was amazing – and that was just the officers and NCOs. The intake of forty to which I was attached was quite something. They were pleasant enough eighteen year olds, but they didn't appear to have any idea about anything in the wide, wide world. At the time there were two wars being fought: the Korean war, which could well have been connected to General MacArthur's bruised ego, although it cost so many American and British servicemen's lives – and the affair in the Malayan Peninsula. Here we were, apparently entitled to slaughter the indigenous population who misguidedly preferred to rule their own country. But of course British property, mainly in the form of the rubber plantations, took precedence over that.

I remember years later reading an article in the *Observer* by Edward Cranshaw about his time as a junior officer in Malaya. They'd been on patrol and had been engaged by some freedom fighters, resulting in the death of two of these zealots. They made their way to the nearest large plantation house to report what had happened. Being an officer, he had been invited into the hallowed edifice for a drink. The other ranks were directed to a dwelling reserved for the native labourers and were given water. When told of the incident, the lady of the house apparently leapt into the air and screamed with delight, grabbed her camera and dashed off to photograph the corpses! It bore a similarity to a tale told on television by Anthony Howard (a former editor of the *New Statesman*) when he described his Suez experiences as a National Serviceman. He told of crossing the Mediterranean from Cyprus in an open landing craft, feeling queasy beyond belief, and being amazed that the officer in charge suddenly sprang into action as they approached Alexandria, stood up in the bows of the craft in true John Wayne (*Sands of Iwo Jima*) stance and exhorted them to 'Come on and give Johnny Gyppo hell!'

We met them. They were everywhere. To them war was fun. What morons! Not one of that intake, through no fault of their own completely uneducated in the ways of the world, had the slightest idea where Korea or Malaya lay on the map. But they were expected to travel to those lands and attempt to slaughter as many of the dissident Orientals as they could. The amazing thing to me was that they seemed to want to do exactly that. Many of them just couldn't wait!

After about a week we were taken by lorry to the firing range at Tyldsley Wood near Pershore. Great excitement. For the first time in their young lives they were allowed to fire rifles in earnest. I allowed myself just one outer, and deliberately missed the target with all my remaining rounds. Two or three of them had done exceptionally well. I remember one lad leaping up and down, with his prestigious target held high, actually shouting 'Yippee, I'm going to be a sniper!' Doubtless he envisaged himself on leave in Worcester in his uniform, with gleaming white blancoed crossed rifles on each forearm creating an impression. Trying not to be unduly cynical, I could imagine proud elderly female relatives beaming, 'Doesn't he look smart in his uniform!' How many people who seem to gain such pleasure from the pageantry of military finery realise that this is just a recruiting display, and that all these red tunics were originally that colour so they wouldn't show the bloodstains quite so obviously. How long our excited young friend would have lasted as a sniper high up alone in the Malayan jungle doesn't bear thinking about.

Two or three days later we were marched into the gymnasium to be addressed by the CO. He was a cartoonist's dream come true. Quite small, with a bristling upper lip and ample circumference, he launched into his tirade. 'Mi mehn,' he puffed, 'Moast of y' hyah will eitha be joinin' the reg'ment in Mallaaayah, or y'll be goin' with the South Staff'rdsheer Reg'ment to Koreaah!' Hardly unexpectedly, his speech was full of lots of crazy phases about 'pride in the regiment', and other similarly banal statements. I'd been conscripted against my will, five years late, to go and fight in what I considered to be an immoral conflict. Why on earth should I feel pride in a regiment into which I'd been press-ganged some ten days before? I was in a madhouse, being berated by an imbecile.

After an evening of fatigues and contemplation, the next morning I reported to the medical reception centre, complaining about pains in my feet. They really did hurt

after all that drill and foot stamping. But I'd grown used to considerable discomfort on Saturday nights after strenuous games of football. I obviously had something wrong with my feet, so I thought it might be an opportune time to investigate. Sometimes in life, quite often in mine, lady luck smiles benignly upon us. The young medical officer was also a National Service man, probably just as passionate about spending two valuable years in an army uniform as I was. Almost without looking up, and basing his judgement solely on my testimony, he murmured, 'Um, no, I don't think you're fit for infantry duties. I'll suggest a transfer to some other branch of the army.' Trying not to display the overwhelming pleasure welling up within me, I made my way back to join the group of people running, stamping, marching and being yelled at on the parade ground below. Later that day I was told that on the following Thursday I would be joining the RASC at Blenheim Barracks, Aldershot.

I nearly sabotaged the whole operation, however. The day before I was due to leave Norton Barracks a runner arrived in the hut during the morning's five minute gap between drill parade and cookhouse duties. 'Is there anyone in here who has played cricket?' he yelled. There was only one arm raised. Mine. 'Get over to the cricket pavilion beyond the parade ground!' he screamed. 'At the double!' I did run, but not at the double. Inside the old wooded pavilion I was kitted out with badly fitting whites and treated like a necessary makeweight. We were fielding, and as we walked out to the middle I was asked whether I bowled, batted or what. I expressed a desire if possible to field close on the leg side. This seemed to be acceptable to the rest of our team, most of whom obviously preferred not to. Nine of my confederates were officers, and a staff sergeant completed the full complement. Actually, the captain, who was also a captain by rank, was quite a pleasant and friendly person. We were arraigned against the Gentlemen of Worcestershire. Ironically, and amazingly, twenty or so years later I was to play quite a few games for the 'Gents' myself, but by the mid-seventies the make-up of the side had altered considerably, and was much more democratic. During the course of their innings I managed to hold onto three quite spectacular catches at short forward square. During tea our captain came up and said, 'I can see you have played before. Where would you like to bat?' I couldn't believe my ears. For the previous few days I had been yelled at, screamed at, and generally belittled and denigrated.

'Thank you, sir', I said. 'I quite fancy opening if that's not stepping on someone's toes.'

'We have a regular opening pair, I'm afraid, but would number three appeal?' he replied. This was even more remarkable. I'd expected 'number eleven and no taps'.

It's all a bit hazy now but I think we were chasing one hundred and thirty odd. When I went to the wicket we were about fifty for one. Wickets began to fall, but I was enjoying myself. I have a crystal clear memory of straight-driving the son of the then chief constable of Worcestershire for six right on to the roof of the RSM's house. Later he actually bowled his 'tweekers' once or twice as an amateur in first class cricket, and I played a few times with him for Pershore in their glory years. Just a few were needed, and I was trying to seal it all and complete my half century with another lofted smite, but was caught on the boundary for forty-eight. After the match the captain came up and asked me about my plans. I got the idea that a job at the barracks might be found for me. I had to tell him I was off the next day. He had the good grace to wish me well.

Chapter Twelve

And so to Aldershot, where I spent two appalling weeks with RASC flashes on my shoulder. There was some mix up about my posting, as it turned out. They apologised to me as I left, but that was after fourteen days of really repressive treatment. The holding company to which I'd been attached was, it seems, a depository for people turfed out of other units for various criminal activities, and the treatment meted out was obviously a form of punishment. Ironically, the inmates were a much greater advertisement for the goodness of the common man than were our jailers.

The nineteenth-century barracks had a wooden floor that had been purposely hacked up with metal spikes. The idea was that, on top of all else, by end of the fourteen days it was to be dead smooth and polished to perfection. We had kit inspections, all laid out with boxed-up bed linen and blankets every morning at 5.30 a.m. We were confined to barracks for the whole two weeks, obviously. Every day we did eight hours of cookhouse fatigues, the evening being spent bulling up our equipment, ironing our uniforms and smoothing out that floor.

It was September and quite warm. Sometimes we were allowed out of the cookhouse steam into the late summer air, but not to laze around. I'd heard about various idiotic military practices, but here at Aldershot in 1952 I experienced two of them at first hand. Painting coal white was one. I did that one. The second task I had heard of, but never really believed. We were lined up outside the

company office and each given a small piece of wood to which a razor blade had been attached. A particularly bovine RSM stood on one side with his pace stick jutting out. He yelled at us to kneel down and systematically hack at the long grass of the lawn outside the company office.

If you stopped for a moment a murderous bellow would erupt. It took about an hour. [

I don't know if all the people unfortunate enough to do National Service share my view, but I bet most of them do. Put bluntly, it was an inoculation against ever having the remotest desire to become a regular soldier.

On about the tenth day I was marched at high speed (there's a military phrase to describe this, but I could never be bothered to remember what it is) to see the personal selection officer. He was actually quite pleasant, and it was he who half-heartedly apologised for the error that had been made. But he did have that ingrained public school attitude. He obviously believed that he was addressing an inferior being. 'You could either stay here and go to OCTU at Buller barracks, or you could go to the Intelligence Corps,' he informed me. 'Actually, I think I'd advise the latter. I think you'd need to cultivate a little more "side" if you wanted to obtain a commission.' He actually said the word 'side'. If I needed convincing, that word above all else alienated me from all things military for life.

In mid-afternoon on the last Sunday at Aldershot, arms deep in greasy suds, there occurred the most tremendous bang you could ever imagine. The building shook and rattled. About a quarter of a mile away Farnborough Air Show had been taking place all week. All the parade grounds were jampacked with parked cars. We had no idea what had happened. To venture outside without permission was probably a capital offence, we reasoned. It was, of course, the infamous crash that took place when John Derry was attempting to break the sound barrier with a low level pass over the crowds as a spectacular finale. Thirty-three people were killed and hundreds more were maimed. Later we were allowed outside, temporarily, for a bit of fresh air, only to be confronted by scores of bandaged and bloodied spectators making their way back to the parked cars.

*****

Two days later I was perched in a rattling old local train as it made its way from Hampshire to Sussex. The relief at leaving Aldershot was tangible. For the rest of my life I've avoided the place like the plague, even making major diversions to keep away. Now here I was, with a rail pass to Uckfield and a bus pass to Maresfield, the School of Military Intelligence. I didn't really know what to expect, but the reality was a revelation. I was convinced that they'd realise they had made another blunder, and I'd be back being dehumanised by morons.

Dropped off at the Chequers, a pub well known to most Intelligence Corps personnel, I made my way to the guard room set among trees – for this was the edge of Ashdown Forest. After the preceding four weeks this was a haven from indignity. We began a three month field security course, which consisted mainly of lectures, even talks by people who'd been at the 1946 Nuremberg war crimes trials – including Sir Hartley Shawcross himself, who lived nearby. In one amusing episode we were trained in the technique of trailing a suspect around a town centre. This took place in Brighton. In films it looks quite simple, but in real life it is virtually impossible as a lone operator. It's so much easier with two. At the culmination of the three months we all went off to a battle training ground at Brandon, on the edge of Thetford forest in Norfolk. The exercise was based on a small estate of houses that had been built in 1939 but never occupied. I was designated the town mayor and was 'imprisoned', locked into a single room in a remote house to await interrogation. I have no recollection of being given any idea of what secret knowledge I was supposed to possess. I can't imagine this really troubled me. After all, this was the army. I didn't lose much sleep over our instructions, just kept my head down and went with the flow. Being in the Intelligence Corps was highly preferable to anything else I'd encountered militarily, so the most sensible strategy was not to rock the boat. It was a cold December that year and that little room was pretty icy. I'd already experienced the wind blowing off the North Sea the previous winter. In the year since then, I'd changed from master of my own destiny to a conscripted hired killer – and all for twenty eight shillings a week.In retrospect it was unbelievable. I knew then what I wanted to return to as soon as was humanly possible. I didn't want to spend a day longer than necessary at the beck and call of anybody else. The army had already made me extremely bitter.

At one end of the room lay a fireplace. Someone had had a fire, for there were a few bits of burnt coal in the hearth. All four walls were painted with a pale emulsion. After an hour boredom set in. I retrieved a nugget of coal embers and started to draw. By the time they came to interrogate me I had covered all four walls. What I actually drew is a bit hazy, but most of it was people, animals, cars, tractors and aeroplanes set against a landscape. I can remember the outline of the Malverns, and May Hill. Of course I included a drawing of myself perched on top of a Fordson Major pulling a pick-up baler, with a queue of traffic behind. There were footballers and cricket scenes. I think it might have been my depiction of land girls in shorts picking apples on ladders that caused the most interest when they all flooded in at dusk.

I stopped the exercise. The officers didn't bother to interrogate me, only to ask questions about the mural. Where was that? What did that bit of farm machinery do? After brewing up they stood around, hands behind backs, discussing it all, like a dozen Dukes of Edinburgh. It could well, in retrospect, have saved my life.

*****

After Christmas embarkation leave the day came when we were loaded onto lorries with our kit bags, off to Tilbury. I don't ever remember being told where we were destined to go, but it could well have been Korea. The Intelligence Corps didn't fare too well in Korea. People just disappeared, notably George Blake, and some were never heard of again. As the convoy approached the guardroom a figure came running out, waving a piece of paper and shouting, 'Is there a Jones 309 on that lorry?'

'Yes,' I yelled, not knowing what was up, but with the feeling that nothing could be worse than eighteen months in a cold and dangerous war zone.

'Get your kit and report to Captain Waters over on the Russian linguists' wing!' he screamed. A piercing scream was the normal way to address another human being, it appeared. I did as I was told and was ushered into Captain Waters' warm, friendly office.

'Ah, Jones,' he said, motioning towards a chair. 'I'm glad we managed to catch you in time. I was up in Brandon before Christmas and saw the drawings you did on those walls. Um, I must declare my interest. I was a farmer's son myself before that last bit of unpleasantness. What I was wondering is . . . can you draw people with clothes on . . .? No, I jest. But I think you could be just the chap we've been looking for. We want to produce some new wall charts and educational aids to help these clever young gentlemen grasp things a little more accurately. Have a cup of tea. How are things down there in the Severn Valley?' He seemed to know quite a bit about me. Perhaps it was that outline of the Malvern Hills. 'What I have in mind is roughly this. You can have that old empty hut behind the coal yard, and I'll keep you supplied with ideas. If you keep your head down nobody will bother you at all. It's Thursday now. We can't do anything till Monday, so if you want to go back to the rolling acres for the weekend that's all right by me.'

Still slightly bemused by what happened I was soon aboard an old green Southdown bus, heading towards Hayward's Heath and two train journeys home. It was amazing. In the course of an hour I'd been rescued from an impending nightmare and here I was, a temporary civilian, heading back to normality. I felt that perhaps the dream would end and I'd be back living the nightmare. Would I be arrested for being AWOL?

Seventy-two hours later I was back, this time in my trusty old Morris series E van. It was a great feeling. Never at any time during the next eighteen months did I wear military uniform when I was among normal people. That meant a great deal to me as I disliked being seen in uniform with an intensity that might be difficult to understand. I was obviously not eighteen years old, so people would assume I was a regular soldier. That horrified me. Having lived through the Second World War I realised that a great many people had made heroic sacrifices,often the final one, in the armed services. But there had also been a great waste of human life. I could see the point of an army to protect my homeland but not to barge around the world as if we owned the place.I think many people still believed for years after 1945 that we really did still run the whole show. I think most of us at Maresfield felt much as I did. None of my friends would ever have thought of going out in the evening to the local pub or down to Brighton in uniform. I suppose this, above all else, symbolised how we felt about being dragooned into being National Servicemen. There was a great longing to get it over and done with.

*****

A few weeks later the notorious east coast floods, in which over three hundred people drowned, took place. We were taken in a convoy of lorries over London Bridge and to Grays in Essex to help those in danger. This took the form of filling sandbags in the bottom of large open barges. It was snowing most of the time, but we were perspiring in our shirtsleeves. In all probability it was a chargeable offence to remove your battledress blouse before the second week in May, but who cared? Those sandbags were badly needed. It was extremely rewarding and most unusual as a soldier to feel that we were doing something worthwhile. Before we left we were thanked profusely by some local dignitary. He obviously meant it.

*****

Captain Waters was as good as his word and there followed eighteen months of the sort of life I'd never dreamt of having in the army. I made a nice snug area to live in at the end of the hut, and spent the days drawing illustrated charts of Russian battle formations, tanks, uniforms, pictures of the adjutant's dog, portraits of famous Soviet marshals (Koniev, Zhukov, Vorishilov, etc.) to hang in the museum. The captain would come down with his latest ideas and spend hours chatting, drinking my tea and talking about farming. He even gave me a fortnight off that summer to help with the haymaking! Whoever heard of such a thing? But more was to come.

Somebody heard that I'd shown promise back home at cricket and football, so I ended up spending at least two days a week playing sport. Both football and cricket were pretty strongly represented. The remarkable thing about both was that neither side ever fielded an officer or a regular soldier! As a footballer I was the typical big, fast, unsophisticated centre forward I'd always been and it worked. We got to the final of the SE Command Cup that year. I was the only one of the eleven who'd never been linked to a league club. The inside left had actually played in the 1950 Amateur Cup Final for Willington at Wembley when they beat the mighty Bishop Auckland. The inside right, John Pretlove, was captain of the combined Oxford and Cambridge sides, Pegasus, when they won the FA Amateur Cup final at Wembley in the late fifties. He was, of course, also a member of the Kent county cricket side under Colin Cowdrey for many seasons. Our large dark haired centre half was the son of one of my childhood heroes, the great Arsenal and England central defender Wilf Copping.

For the semi-final (at Maresfield) the whole camp had to turn out on a bitterly cold day. It was the only time I ever played when the entire touchline was occupied by spectators. I won't say supporters because most of them would sooner have been huddled round a stove. They all had to wear their greatcoats (many for the first and only time). I remember thinking from out on the pitch that it looked like Napoleon's retreat from Moscow. In the first ten minutes I missed three open goals. The crowd knew enough about the game to start chanting 'come on the ten men': it was years before the law to allow substitutes came in. I got worse, but we managed to win. I missed the final, alas, as a result.

There were about six or seven of the cricket team who eventually played first class cricket. Playing all over south-east England was very enjoyable. Our star fast bowler was frequently away playing first class cricket for Combined Services. He was a Lancastrian called Colin Smith, one of two brothers on the county staff at Old Trafford. He was well over six feet in height and with a lithe whippy action. As the designated wicketkeeper I found myself standing at least a full pitch length behind the stumps! Often the ball was still going up as it arrived.For added security I also indulged in the old practice of tying the third and fourth fingers of my gloves together to avoid damage.He had a long curling run to the wicket, with a considerable drag in his back foot. It was quite a spectacle to behold.

Many years later I became quite friendly with Colin's county captain at Lancashire, the likeable Geoff Edrich. Geoff was cricket coach at Cheltenham College after his county cricket days and played a bit of local stuff around the area. He never ever mentioned that he had endured four years as a prisoner of war after the fall of Singapore. He was one of the very rare ones who had lasted into old age – but he was a pretty tough character, and was proud of his farming background in rural Norfolk. I recall talking to him about Colin and Geoff surprised me by suggesting that he was quite a bit faster than his much more famous opening bowling partner, the great Brian Statham. Colin Smith went on to Cambridge after demobilisation and became a famous architect, winning many awards. The last time I saw him mentioned in print I was pleased to read, but not surprised, that he had become Professor Sir Colin Stanford Smith. Good for him.

Just one more cricket story. I was asked by one of the Intelligence Corps team, John Pretlove, if I'd turn out in his stead in a weekend club match on the county ground at Tunbridge Wells. I duly turned up in the old van and was introduced to my fellow players for the day. We batted first. I remember it being a very warm late August day in 1953. Our openers were in great touch. I had been designated number three, but it didn't look as if I was even going to get a tap. You could place the date because I can remember lying on the grass and listening to a commentary of one of the last ever 'Ulster' 500cc motorcycle Grand Prix. I remember that it was won by the Australian Ken Campbell, on I believe a Moto-Guzzi. Eat your heart out, Leslie Welch. Anyway, about five to five and presumably tea, one of our openers was out. We were about 280 for 1. I fully expected a declaration. Perhaps he felt he ought to let me, the guest player, at least have a bat.

Arriving at the crease I was informed that there was one ball left in the over. The bowler came thundering in: he was quite a useful 'military medium'. Heading towards me was a straight half volley. I suppose I thought, 'This is all a bit pointless, no sense in blocking it, even if it is your first ball.' So I put my left leg slightly out towards mid-on and fortunately hit it with unbelievably perfect timing. It felt like hitting a golf ball. I don't think they ever found it. Right over the sightscreen it went, bouncing on and on. On the first ball of the next over I was the non-striker and was run out by a distance. I think we declared and took tea. It wasn't until later that I began to think this could have been an almost unique innings in a serious game of cricket. I suppose it could have been done elsewhere or since, but certainly not often. I had faced one ball, scored six runs and was out. Mr Frindall, how about it?

*****

The whole set up at Maresfield was amazing, in retrospect. I have no idea how they selected those who were eventually destined for the Intelligence Corps. But there was a strange temperamental similarity to the personnel chosen. Perhaps the fact that I had been self-employed before call-up had some bearing on their decision. (As another example, I remember being astonished to find on my first day at Maresfield that the occupant of the adjoining bed had been a unicyclist in a circus. Unbelievably he rejoiced in the name Pedlar.) Without giving away too many state secrets (it is more than fifty years ago, after all), one of the basic requirements for Intelligence personnel working 'in the field' was an ability to fend for yourself. This was in total contrast to being a normal military conscript, being browbeaten incessantly until you reacted like an automaton when orders were screamed in your direction. Nobody had any interest in promotion or anything remotely regimental – the Russian linguists especially. Almost all of them had spent eighteen months at the Joint Services School for Linguists at Bodmin. To a man they'd loved Cornwall, not being in a real army, wearing civilian clothes, and heading for the coast at Newquay, Padstow, Port Isaac and Polzeath at weekends. They'd emerged with degree-standard Russian, from scratch, which was quite an achievement. When they arrived and had to wear uniforms again they cut very strange figures. I never really knew many of them closely: I was in my hut and away from everything, after all. But they wore little name tags, and although this probably seems like 'name dropping' it isn't. I didn't really know them: we talked in the Naafi, that was about all. They all seemed to want to become journalists, without exception.

There was a very thin, untidy one with round metal glasses who talked with a Yorkshire accent, named 'Bennett A.'. I met him some years ago at a literary festival. When I held my book out for him to sign I said out of the corner of my mouth, 'What does the word Maresfield do to you?' He jumped a bit and said, 'Christ, were you there too? I hated the army. I hope you did?' I grinned, nodded and went on my way. After fifty-odd years you begin to doubt your memory, but I'm pretty certain I can recall a name tag identifying 'Frayn M.', also 'Tomalin N.': he was unfortunately killed in the Six Days War when reporting for the *Sunday Times*). Among others were Tom O'Brien, who later became Tom Springfield, with a famous sister named Mary (or 'Dusty'), Peter Woods, who became a BBC newscaster, and Simon Oates, who became an actor and star of the cult seventies TV drama *Doomwatch*. We became quite good friends, and he would borrow my old van occasionally to hit the nightspots of Brighton. After demob I read that he became quite famous as a stand-up comedian. It followed, for he used to amuse me greatly. Another, later to change his name from 'Cornwell D.' became John le Carré, but I certainly didn't know him socially. Some of them became close friends – in particular Ben Wright, whom I knew from shared experiences on the cricket field. He was already a minor counties player for Bedfordshire and also a scratch golfer. Later he became deputy sports editor to Peter Wilson on the *Daily Mirror*, before leaving to become editor of *Golf World*. For years he was part of the ITV golf team, before leaving these shores to work in America with ABC. We corresponded once or twice over the years but never actually met again. Someone I knew quite well was Gareth Powell. His father was a poor law officer and small farmer in rural Flintshire. In 1957 I bumped into Gareth in Fleet Street. He was, he claimed, hard up and working all hours at a publishing house in Long Acre. We talked for hours, comparing notes. About seven years later he suddenly appeared on Eamonn Andrews' TV chatshow, introduced as 'Britain's newest millionaire' (when that really meant something). I read that he had somehow acquired various publishing houses, including the American paperback imprints Signet and Mentor. I don't know if this is true, but it's what I read! Jokingly, I wrote to him, congratulating him on his good fortune. He replied immediately (it was 1964, not 2004) and invited me up to his offices. He apparently had many people I knew from the past working in his company, which I thought was quite a good effort. I didn't actually go to visit him in the end, as it seemed a bit like trying to jump on someone else's bandwagon.

Among some of us at this time the bible was Jaroslav Hasek's famous anti-war treatise *The Good Soldier Svejk*. Years later I remember attending a talk by one of my literary heroes, Joseph Heller. I had purchased another copy of *Catch 22* especially to obtain the great man's signature. I stood in line and held out the book, which he duly signed. Our eyes met for a moment. I'm not a great one for mouthing inanities on such occasions, so I murmured an almost inaudible thanks and that was that. I could have told him how very much I always wished he'd written his great work some years before 1958, as I'm sure it would have pushed Svejk off the pedestal.But I said nothing, of course. Three weeks later he was dead.

*****

Demobilisation eventually arrived. Those two years have always seemed the longest of my whole life. My stepfather had left, and my brother and I began to farm as Jones Bros – with little capital and a very annoying bank manager. About a month later we received a notice from on high to the effect that Church Farm, Queenhill, had been designated to be the site of the proposed M50 bridge over the Severn, a viaduct and motorway – which would in effect cut off the farm from the farmhouse, farm buildings and orchard. But they couldn't say when, just 'some time soon'. Every month surveyors arrived and hammered little white pegs into the fields. As soon as they'd gone, the cows sniffed enquiringly at them and kicked them out of the ground with great dexterity. Back would come the surveyors. . . .

I must admit I was beginning to think that someone somewhere had got it in for me! It wasn't helped by the fact that in 1955 the Severn flooded and for the first time in living memory in midsummer. We were used to winter floods (four or five a year) but this ruined everything: about sixty acres of mowing grass, fourteen acres of barley and seven acres of potatoes. I remember when we combined that field of barley. There was a great cloud of (mud) dust rising about a hundred feet in the air, like an atomic bomb's mushroom cloud. It was a complete loss, of course.

Chapter Thirteen

Not long after I returned to civilian life and that wonderful feeling of being master of my own destiny again, unaffected by the insanity of pigmy autocrats, I had the first of two rather satisfying confrontations with the blood sports brigade.

I was deep in a reverie about the joy of being free again when my grassland trek was brought to an annoyingly abrupt conclusion by the sound of thundering hooves and baying voices. It was the local hunt, making their muddy way across the previously peaceful parkland.

I was approaching the tall metal gate that led into eight acres of winter wheat. The neat lines of parallel shoots covered the entire field, boding well for the next year's harvest. Then an enormous horse reined up at my side, almost colliding with me. Sitting astride this snorting beast was an absurdly pompous, small man in a hunting pink jacket straight out of a musical comedy. This pretentious idiot gestured toward the gate with his crop and bellowed, 'I say, open that gate will you, Tommy!' Perhaps it was his military appearance and manner than caused my sudden fury. I had learnt over a turbulent early life that self control is all-important in life's little incidents, but this was too much. I had endured enough of such martinet behaviour over the past two years, and had always been unable to respond as I would have dearly wished. This was very different. This was land I partly owned. As far as I was concerned he and his cohorts were uninvited trespassers, engaged in an ancient and barbaric pastime that I detested.

'Open the bloody gate yourself, you pompous bastard,' I countered. 'Don't you feel any shame, any of you? We certainly don't want you charging over our land. Don't you realise you're not welcome?' He snorted something about my being an insolent young pup who needed a good horsewhipping, and aimed his mount at the lowest point of the adjacent hedge, knocking a considerable hole in the leafy barrier. The remaining thirty or forty riders crashed through the gap that he had made, none of them giving me a single glance. I didn't see anyone I knew. Most of the female contingent, looking foolishly masculine in their regulation raiment, bore the appearance of being down from town for a day out. They galloped away across the pale green shoots of growing corn, leaving a dark brown strip, some thirty yards wide, of churned-up soil. It looked as if it had been traversed by a madman with a tractor and a gang of disc harrows. The gap they had left in the hedge was now at least eight feet wide.

I ran back to the farm buildings that lay two fields away to the north. Here I grabbed some stakes, a roll of barbed wire, some strainers and everything that I needed to repair the devastation. Throwing it all into a trailer hitched to a nearby tractor I sped back to the scene of devastation. The herd of steers that I'd feared would beat me to the scene were heading that way at a trot. About ninety minutes later the gap was safely sealed. Doing such a job single handed is not the easiest of tasks, but it held.

Out of curiosity I drove the tractor down to a spot where the hunt, almost without exception, failed to close a particularly important gate. It was open. At this point the farm ended and the ancient drive up to the manor house in the trees passed from our land to that of the big house, Pull Court. For years this had been the home of the mother of Richard Seaman, who became famous in the late '30s as a driver in the all-conquering Mercedes-Benz motor racing team. When he was killed in Belgium just before the outbreak of war his mother became a recluse, and the driveway became overgrown and virtually impenetrable. Unfortunately the driveway wasn't inaccessible to cattle. Often our animals would gain entrance, usually when the main gate was left ajar by some thoughtless person. Something approaching panic would then ensue. All the cattle would be driven home and corralled for a couple of days in the yards. This was because there were numerous yew trees in this overgrown driveway. Yew is lethal to cattle if they eat it and then drink water. Kept away from water for two days most of them usually survive. If they do succumb it's not a pretty sight: the animal becomes distended and eventually splits open. It's quite a gory spectacle. The farm on the far side of the big house suffered more from this than we did.

I have a clear memory of walking through the low branches and bushes that had once lined a formal driveway, and of coming upon a particularly gruesome tableau. It had been snowing heavily, as it usually did in those winters immediately after the war. In a clearing were fifteen of our neighbour's heifers, some in calf, lying on the snow-covered earth. They had had their lethal drink: snow. It was barely daylight, which probably added to the distressing nature of the scene. They were all dead. All of them were spilt open, and there was blood everywhere. Everywhere was blood, excrement, entrails. It's still as clear in my memory as it was on that bitterly cold morning over fifty years ago. With this returning to haunt me in all its gory detail, I now know for sure why I find the much-lauded and greatly publicised pop art image of recent times so unsettling. I know I should accept modernism as a form of progress, but that depiction of a sliced-up cow in formaldehyde seems so perverse and unpleasant. There must be other subjects, surely. Or does it just show lack of imagination, of never having lived outside the confined inbred world of art college chatter?

My second meeting with another branch of the animal-slaughtering fraternity happened a few months after my confrontation with Colonel Blimp and his fence-destroying friends. One day, returning home from a bit of a ramble around the Severnside meadows, I crossed one of the inner fields to look at the height of the water in the local brook. Often, if you approached the little waterway with caution, you could be lucky

otter at play.

88

enough to observe otters, which were quite common in those far-off days. Rather like young lambs, they seemed to have a desire to indulge in playful activities.

It's quite common in late spring to see lambs playing. In the parkland beside the church, where the sequoias decorated the pastures rather incongruously, one tree had fallen some years before and was positioned rather like a large praying insect. Most of the branches had been trimmed off, while the tip of the tree rested on the turf. Every year a new batch of spring lambs played the same game as their predecessors had done. In an almost choreographed routine a line of lambs ran along the fallen tree trunk, jumping off at the highest point near the base, a not inconsiderable height, and then trotting round in formation, before leaping up onto the far end.

I grew quite fond of individual lambs, as I did of other farm animals. So many of them seemed to have an individual intelligence. They even looked at you as if they understood. Sometimes I wonder if I was ever cut out to be a business-like farmer. When the batches of fat lambs or

store cattle were loaded up and dispatched to the abattoir I would feel a great sadness. Often I found some other task so that I didn't witness their departure. I suppose that's why lots of people prefer cereal farming to livestock husbandry.

Otters were very similar in their habits to spring lambs, in that they had a great desire to play happily in the sunshine. I realise that I've used the past tense in describing them. It must be a good forty-five years since I've seen an otter in the flesh, but they are thankfully returning to many areas of Britain. That day I was hoping to see a few otters at play. If you were lucky you could hide behind a bush and watch as they slid joyously down the steep earthen bank, landing with a splash in the brook. They'd then bound up to the top and repeat the action, and their slides would eventually become smooth and muddy and wet. When surprised they would leap into the brook and disappear.

Unfortunately there were no otters to be seen that day so I began the long trudge back to the buildings up on the higher land, so I could get on with the daily grind. As I approached the gravel drive that led to the church I became aware of various dilapidated vehicles parked on the grass and about twenty dogs. About ten pretty unsavoury looking men were milling around, looking as if they were about to move off somewhere with their moth-eaten animals.

'Can I help you?' I enquired. 'Who are you anyway?' The obvious leader of the motley crew complete with about a week's stubble, looked up and proudly announced that they were the Ross-on-Wye Otter Hounds and were looking for their quarry on this particular stretch of water today – almost as if he was dispensing a favour. It was probably as well that I towered over him, otherwise things could have got a bit fraught. 'Well,' I informed him, 'you're not welcome here, I can tell you that right now. Why kill them, for God's sake? I could spend hours watching them.' He looked at me as if I was mad – but it worked. They loaded up their mongrels and departed. It was some years before otters eventually became an endangered species, not before time. I often wondered about the validity of their claims that day. For all I knew they were badger baiters intent on a bit of daytime sport.

*****

Some quite amusing things happened during those two years, although most of it was soul destroying. On one occasion the local parson walked across from the church, obviously intent on conversing about something he deemed to be important. He had been a naval officer in the war who had seen the light in the years thereafter. By the time he became the local vicar I think the light was beginning to fade. He was a very nice man, and when asked whether his belief in a deity was as strong as ever he mumbled something about still being in a position to do good. Some time later I think he resigned. My brother and I were planting kale in a field some two hundred yards from the church when the vicar hailed us with a wave of his arm. 'I wonder', he began, 'if you'd have any objection to my bringing my flock [his ageing aunt] over here on Sunday. It's Rogation Sunday, and it's blessing the crops time.' There was a slight pause, then I heard my brother pipe up in reply, 'Yes, that'll be OK, Reverend. It'll save us putting any fertiliser on it.' The vicar burst into spontaneous laughter and my heart warmed to him: he was human after all.

*****

By this time I was married, and in due course my son Martin was born. His early life was fraught with medical crises. First he accidentally drank from a tin of tractor vapourising oil. Later he was to endure a horrendous experience with a gangrenous appendix, which necessitated seven weeks in the prehistoric Gloucester Royal Infirmary. When he miraculously recovered he bore a resemblance to a Belsen survivor. Eventually he went to the University of East Anglia to study physics – and today he travels the globe as a hydraulics expert, specialising in the use of hydraulics in Formula One motor racing. His daughter Alice is taking the first steps in her quest to become a psychologist.

Some years later his sister Karen came along, a happy, healthy soul, who, with husband Terry has in turn brought forth a 'pigeon pair'. Kate, my grand-daughter, is reading music at Birmingham University, and young Josh is showing considerable prowess as an oarsmen.

*****

91

In the autumn of 1955, after the summer flood and other misfortunes, the time approached when I had to report to Maresfield for my two weeks of reserve military training. [051] An inner fury was slowly building up within me. Times were rough, things were tight, we were busy, and I really did not see why or indeed how I could have two weeks away. Times were already difficult enough. On the Saturday morning on which I was due to set off, still in my old ex-GPO van, on the 140 mile trip to Sussex, something happened that made me rebel against the stupidity of it all. At about eight o'clock a large beast just keeled over and died. Nobody really knew why, so we rang the vet. Waiting for him to arrive, I looked at my case packed for a fortnight's pointless time-wasting exercise and suddenly made a decision. I sent a telegram to the military powers down in the southeast. It read: 'SUSPECTED ANTHRAX ON FARM, PLEASE ADVISE ME AS TO PROCEDURE REGARDING AER TRAINING DUE TO COMMENCE LATER TODAY.' Within about an hour I received a reply: 'STAY AWAY, WILL ADVISE FUTURE PLANS LATER.' It turned out not to be anthrax, but I never went near a military establishment again. You win some, sometimes. But we had just lost a valuable beast, so it had its downside.

Chapter Fourteen

n late summer the cows would be in the distant river meadows. So many mornings in the misty dawn I have been down there to collect them for milking, thinking what a marvellous scene it was to behold. (I've painted if from memory since.) About thirty to forty cows lying down in a sea of mist with just their heads and necks visible, some asleep, some chewing the cud. At the first call they'd all start lumbering to their feet, often breaking wind and exuding the usual hosepiping excrement.

We had a friendly old pure Hereford cow that had horns almost as long as the fabled longhorns of yesteryear – they were just like handlebars. Incidentally, why are people so impressed by Duchamp's sculpture? It has always amazed me. I remember connecting these images as a young child: the similarity between a bovine skull and a racing bicycle seat had seemed obvious long before I had even heard of Duchamp. This cow (Priscilla, I recall) always managed to look stupid: I think it was the big white face, although she could have been stupid too.

One morning I peered through a gap in the hedge and there she was, fast asleep, mist up to her chin as she lay. In perfect symmetry she had a carrion crow perched on each horn, on the horizontal bits.

Later she gave us an even more bizarre image. She'd had her calf weaned and the night had been full of distant bellowing from way down by the river. Later, as I was thinking of arising, a familiar deafening bellow came from below my bedroom window. There was Priscilla, by the closed gate into the yard, bellowing like mad. Plaintive answers were coming from a far-off shed. Perfectly balanced on her enormous horns was a very substantial five-barred gate. Cows have very strong necks. Behind her were about thirty cows all ready to be tied up and relieved of their milk.

Another image remains from those distant late summer mornings down by the river. It wasn't always misty, and it was common on clearer days to see a long pair of ears suddenly appear in the foot high 'aftermath'. An eye would gleam and whoosh off across the field at the most

amazing speed: a hare. I can't think of a more pleasing sight than a hare in full flight. It is utterly beyond me why anybody should want to grab a gun and kill it. Is it some defect in the human psyche?

Another cow-related incident jogs my memory. It was Easter Saturday. The phone rang. It was our neighbour who farmed on the far bank of the Severn. 'I don't want to worry you, but I seem to have got one of your cows,' he began, obviously rather amazed. It was an unusually dry spring and we'd put the cows down into the river meadows. It appeared that a heavily in-calf cow had slipped down the steep riverbank, probably down an angler's steps, and being unable to get back up had swum across the sixty foot river. She was now over on the far side. Thanking our neighbour, we rushed down to see what had happened, only to be ·confronted by a great bovine moon face staring up at us from the mud below. She'd done the return trip! One of us stayed with her, hoping she wouldn't swim off again, while the other ran back to fetch a tractor and a rope. Eventually we managed to get the rope round her mighty horns, selected a better gradient and, after a lot of effort and sodden clothes, we hauled her up onto the field above. She didn't have any great objection to being hauled along by a tractor, it seemed, so to be on the safe side we dragged her about fifty yards into another meadow – without a river bank. She seemed OK and began to chew the cud, so we left her to calm down. Later that day an inspection revealed a contented cow licking her newly born calf.

Chapter Fifteen

In all the descriptions of livestock and implements, it's easy to overlook the role of domestic animals on farms. Most farms support quite a crowd of feral cats and, of course, sheepdogs almost always make themselves useful.

One of my first memories is of peacocks disporting themselves on the long roof of the cowshed, showing off their fanned tail feathers and emitting their raucous call. Suddenly they were gone, to be replaced by a vast array of farm cats, sunning themselves in an almost military formation. At one stage my father counted twenty-seven. They appeared to be descended from the large father figure who always placed himself in the centre of the formation on the roof. He was a very imposing animal, a peculiar brownish tabby colour but with lots of white about his person. He had a white chest and stomach, four white paws, a white tip to his tail and enough white about his face to appear alive and intelligent. All his descendants were very similar – the same basic colour, with varying amounts of white. On a summer evening they were quite a spectacle.

Ten or fifteen years later the farm was populated by a new generation of similar cats. The tamer ones would sit in the doorways of the cowshed and watch what was going on. One or two became very adept at accepting a stream of warm milk that was sent in their direction straight from the cow's udder, their minute pink tongues working overtime. When milking finished, as we carried the milking machines the eighty yards to the dairy, they would all follow in a bunch, periscopic tails waving rhythmically. They knew from long experience that sustenance was in the offing. Small troughs or even an upturned rusty old churn lid would be filled with foaming milk, and they were soon slurping away merrily.

As feral cats are usually kleptomanically inclined they were not allowed into the farmhouse, but lived in the farm buildings, where they decimated the rodent population. One particular female became an especial pet. She was completely brown tabby in colour, not unlike a rabbit in fact. Early in her life she managed to sit on the remnants of a broken chlorine bottle, and soon only had a stump of a tail: to all intents and purposes she looked like a native of the Isle of Man. Two or three years later she miraculously survived the indignity of being run over by the small trailer that transported five or six full milk churns out to the stand on the lane beyond the farm. Temporarily she was allowed into the house and spent a week hovering between life and death on an old blanket in a basket by the fireplace in the scullery, being fed shots of whisky. But she was as tough as nails and was soon back outside catching her fair share of mice. She, of course, became known as Bobtail – and lived until well into her teens.

On long summer evenings, usually on Sundays, I often walked around the farm, noting what needed attention and how the crops were faring. Almost invariably Bobtail took it upon herself to join this mile long tramp. Unlike dogs, cats aren't keen on the idea of trotting along dutifully at your heels. They are, after all, completely different in temperament. A backwards glance would show her to be perhaps fifty yards behind, examining something intently; then suddenly there would be a sound of pounding feet and she would rush past at full speed and into the distance, way ahead. There she would sit and wait, feigning a complete lack of interest in human activity, before repeating the action again, on and on, all around the farm. I've heard of other cats that did exactly the same thing. They're strange animals.

We had some memorable farm dogs. Before the war my father had bought a sheepdog from a man who bred and trained them for sheepdog trials somewhere in distant Wales. Dog, as he was always known, was almost white and quite large, but he was not an Old English sheepdog. The story was that he was a reject as far as sheepdog trials had been concerned, but my father had taken pity on him and thought he had been maltreated. He was undoubtedly cowed when he first arrived, but quickly became a great favourite. I have a clear memory of him doing his party trick, which was to 'hurdle' (very much in the style of a racehorse) a five-barred gate at speed. He would be going so fast that he was just a grey blur. My father got him to do this to impress friends and visitors, and even tried, unsuccessfully, to capture the act on film, with a still camera. I don't think he'd heard of 'panning'.

There's another incident I recall concerning Dog. We had a local postman of long standing who'd been told that his beloved spaniel Rip would not be welcome at his new address after he retired. My father suggested that we'd have Rip, and the postman could come and see him when he wanted. But there was a problem as we already had Dog. Rip would have to be tied up and live in a kennel for a week or two. This plan was put into practice, but the poor animal looked so sad that my father took pity on him and had the bright, but flawed, idea of tying the two dogs together with a four or five foot length of rope between their collars. Dog would be able to show Rip around his new surroundings, or that was the idea. We all lined up at the top of the hill by the house and the dogs were duly released. Barking joyously in unison they ran furiously down the hill and out into the home orchard. Unfortunately they decided to go either side of a fence stake. We held our breath. They must have been travelling at something approaching twenty miles per hour – and there was a sickening thud as they collided beyond the stake, head to head, like prong-horned antelopes in combat. As we rushed down to disentangle them there was a lot of pulling and barking, and long before we got anywhere near them they'd extricated themselves from the fence and were away again. Only this time Dog had a long piece of rope attached to an empty collar trailing behind him. Trotting along behind was a rather confused spaniel with its ears still facing forward. Before anybody could reach them they were gone, and it was more than a

day later that they returned. For some years they lived happily together, without the rope.

In later years we had a beautiful black and white border collie who appeared to be more intelligent than many human beings. He could bring a flock of sheep up into the yard all by himself. It was possible to look out into a bit of deserted parkland, point and say 'go and get 'em, Turpin,' and he'd be away.] A few minutes later the sheep would arrive and there, quietly trotting this way and that behind them, would be Turpin with his laughing face, tongue wagging away. The thing was he was so calm, with hardly a bark ever to be heard. He never upset his charges. I've also known him, when left to guard the flock in the yard while we adjourned for lunch, let them go past him into the field, only to bring them back in before we returned to our tasks of clipping and 'maggotting'. (The tasks we did as farmers!)

Chapter Sixteen

The authorities began to talk about a starting date for the construction of the motorway, the viaduct over the river meadows and the bridge over the Severn. We felt hopeless. Nobody was the slightest bit interested in buying our farm as an entity, it seemed. There was interest from various neighbours in taking odd fields, but that was all.

In late 1956 our noble government got itself involved in the disgraceful business over the Suez Canal. I was still an army reservist. I can remember my seething resentment that I could possibly be asked to risk my life to preserve Lord Salisbury's Suez Canal share money. Or worse still, that I would be a part of reinstating the deposed playboy King Farouk on Egypt's throne. Of course in rural Worcestershire the general opinion, if anyone ever gave it prolonged thought, was that we were in the right. 'My country right or wrong, and let's go and knock hell out of the "Gyppos".' Our uncooperative bank manager, one of the old school and a pillar of the local Tory hierarchy, gave me a severe lecture over the phone about my attitude to the whole affair. He was giving yet another ultimatum about something or other, exerting more pressure on a sale, when we got talking about the international situation. I said that as a reservist I might well be asked to don the dreaded uniform again, and observed that I would consider mutiny before fighting over Suez. The effect was electrifying. The phone practically exploded. It was the ghost of Field Marshal Haig himself. The bank manager had never been in the army, of course, but he knew what my reaction should be if I were ordered to rally to the colours.

I often wonder if life would have been different if we'd been luckier with our choice of bank manager. I doubt it really. Subsequent years confirmed my distrust of all banks. If you need money they refuse point blank, but when you eventually accumulate a little capital and property, through no help of any bank, they fall over themselves with offers of loans for all manner of absurd projects. In years that are tight they send a letter informing you that you're overdrawn and charge you a further £25 for the information. The logic is unbelievable.

Eventually in early November (was it Bonfire Night?) we sold the farm by auction in a Gloucester hotel. We gave it away, but I suppose we had little choice. The price we obtained, £8,500 for a large and picturesque farmhouse, many buildings and 135 acres of first-class Severnside alluvial plain land, was criminal. Not all that many years later it was worth £200,000. Today, who knows . . . a million?

Over the years I've tried not to be bitter about that motorway. I've tried to keep looking ahead cheerfully, but it's not always been easy.

Chapter Seventeen

n the depths of winter, pre-Christmas 1956, we had the farm sale. That was twice in sixteen years. Again, everything was laid out in rows in the same field. It was not such an extensive sale but it still hurt. The emptiness afterwards, and the realisation that this time we really were leaving the old place forever.

Shortly after Christmas we were all in Canada. My brother spent fifteen years there working for the Canadian government in Ottawa and Nova Scotia, then for many years overseeing the stockyards of Winnipeg. We went on a pre-First World War Cunarder called the *Scythia*. It was about twenty thousand tons with one tall smoke stack, unlike the *Titanic*, which was larger and had four. . . . Leaving Southampton in early January, destined for New York, we quickly encountered some wild and enormous seas, and more or less ground to a halt. In the middle of one particularly violent night the ship's bells began to ring violently, but luckily it wasn't the call to abandon ship. Sometimes one is so glad for small mercies. For thirty-six hours we stopped in mid-Atlantic with waves of forty feet towering over the shuddering hulk. Frequently the whole ship seemed to slide down into the troughs. Everything rattled alarmingly. During those thirty-six hours it barely got light. Reading about it afterwards, I saw it described as the worst Atlantic storm for forty years. Whether or not that was the case is, I suspect, open to doubt – they probably say that every year. But it certainly felt pretty bad when you were out there.

Eventually, after what should have been an eight day voyage to New York, we limped into Halifax, Nova Scotia, after fourteen days at sea. Various things were done to the old ship before we made the remainder of the trip down past Boston and Cape Cod to New York. Now the sea was like a millpond. I remember going up on deck as we approached our destination. It was barely light and bitterly cold, but there before us was one of those spectacular images that lasts for a lifetime. The sea was flat, there was an amazingly pink dawn sky and wisps of mist clung to the surface of the water. Gradually the ethereal pale blue silhouette of Manhattan and its towering skyscrapers hove into view. The Cunard docks were totally encrusted with sheet ice. I hadn't realised that it could get this cold in New York. Surely it was on the same latitude as Madrid? Life was full of surprises.

There followed a few months of quite traumatic experiences. Stupidly, I hadn't made enough enquiries about the possibilities open to me in this new land. I suppose I thought I'd manage to get work of some sort – after all I'd spent eighteen months in uniform working to all intents and purposes as a commercial artist. Some of my output had even been used by the War Office. I quickly learnt that most Canadian magazines at that time were of American origin with small Canadian inserts. All the famous strips were drawn in New York or Chicago. I got to meet Al Beaton, who was then one of the most famous political cartoonists in Canada, with a daily spread in the *Toronto Globe and Mail*, if my memory serves me right. I know his office was on King Street. He was an exceptionally pleasant man and talked to me for ages. He was about to retire and couldn't wait to get back to his native British Columbia. Al had it all worked out – and aimed to spend his retirement salmon fishing on his beloved Fraser river. I showed him some samples of my work that I'd taken along with me. He was apparently quite impressed and even complimentary. 'Seems to me you're in the wrong place,' he explained. 'You ought to have tried London, England, first. I bet you'd get a stack of work there!'

What I did know was that I had no intention of becoming a farm worker again, on some Canadian holding. I'd done my time as a 'sod-buster', I felt. Anything but that, within reason. I began to feel extremely foolish. Even so, some of the things that happened to me during my search for work in the sub-zero (fahrenheit) temperatures of a Canadian winter still make me smile. It was so bitterly cold that sometimes a quick dive inside the concourse of Toronto's Union station would be impossible to resist. But after I had sat for a few minutes on a bench a large Canadian mountie would loom up and move any vagrants, such as me, out into the icy snow. It felt like Skid Row. I also remember that Fats Domino was playing on every jukebox in every café to which I adjourned for a few minutes' respite from the bitter cold. 'Blue Monday' boomed out from juke boxes everywhere.

On one occasion I made my way to an employment agency in the Spadina area, out toward the western fringes of Toronto. I forget whether Spadina was an Italian ghetto or if it was predominantly populated by Ukranians, but I do recall that a high proportion of the buildings in those days were of wood, and there were quite frequent conflagrations. 'Four Alarm' blazes were not that uncommon. I have a clear memory of hearing a great clamour far off, and before long an enormous articulated fire engine, all vertical barking exhausts, roared around a corner with bells clanging, all hell let loose. It was right out of an early Keystone Kops movie. Men were hanging on to the ladders grimly, some even swinging out from the machine, feet not touching any part of it.

I found the employment agency on about the third floor, and was shown into an interview room. An enormous uniformed man sat behind a desk; a small notice informed me that I was in the presence of 'Eugene P. Koussevitzky'. He offered a friendly hand, bade me sit down and began to write down my personal details.

'Name?' he enquired.

'Jones,' I replied.

He looked up, scratched his head and said, 'Hell, Mac, how d'ya spell that?!' If you're born with a name like Jones, especially west of the River Severn, this is the most unlikely question ever to be asked, I can tell you. Perhaps he was joking – but I doubt it.

Eventually it was back on the train to New York, this time through a greener landscape. In January there had been virtually no grass to be seen, just a blanket of snow and occasionally a glimpse of dead vegetation and brown earth. And then it was onto another Cunarder, this time a larger and more modern vessel, the *Britannic*.

It was a dispiriting return, with very little money left and still no job, or, for that matter, any plans at all. I remember as we approached Cobh off Cork, in the first light of dawn, groups of quite ancient men gathered against the rail, pointing. Some were crying. They had been away so long. Many of them looked not unlike Victor McGlaglen or Ward Bond.

I suppose subconsciously I may have been thinking that I was returning to the old familiar homestead. After all, twice in my life I'd been away for prolonged periods, only to return. But I knew this was not the case, of course. Our home now belonged to a stranger. It had been partitioned off and bulldozers were ripping everything asunder. All twenty-two acres of orchard disappeared quite early in the proceedings. To go anywhere near the place was too painful – and it was forty-eight years later that I eventually made my one and only return visit, to discover it was a conglomeration of barn conversions. The cowshed was a bungalow, and the granary, main hay barn and stable block were all separate residences.

But after almost half a century it didn't seem to matter any more. The owner of the farmhouse, who had invited us to visit, couldn't have been more gracious or welcoming, and I left feeling quite a warm glow inside. The old place was in good hands and I had no intention of ever returning.

Chapter Eighteen

uring the following three weeks I spent every possible hour drawing sample pages of realistic action comic strips, trying to perfect a style. It was quite a challenge. I'd never been an aficionado of comics: although I'd read them at a young age, I'd graduated to novels by the time I first donned long trousers. In my early youth I'd been a voracious reader, quickly tiring of gung-ho tales of derring-do. Aged about fifteen I discovered John Steinbeck. All my

— GEOFF JONES —

life I've considered some of the scenes depicted in *The Grapes of Wrath* as being among the greatest descriptive passages in the English language. The first chapter is truly marvellous. I remember reading it and being instantly hooked. This was something I'd never encountered before. I have an ancient audio tape of the legendary Studs Terkel reading the famous chapter describing migrants on Highway 66 (I think it's chapter twelve). Perhaps it's Studs' creaky old voice, but it seems like a completely truthful description of life in those desperate years in the Dust Bowl, as those migrants toiled westwards on their ramshackle conveyances. I only have to switch it on and the shivers go off the top of my head.

In Canada I had admired such realistic comic-strip artists as Alex Raymond, John Prentice and Ken Bald. I didn't read them, I just liked the drawings! These people were practising the style that I intended to mimic. It was going to be hard work. [

Eventually, armed with half a dozen sample boards, drawn 'half-up' as the term has it, I set off like Dick Whittington for the capital. I certainly didn't expect the streets to be paved with gold – but I must have been very lucky. The second artists' agency that I visited, in a tall block off Chancery Lane, actually gave me both encouragement and a small job to do. Dear old Dan Kelleher of Temple Art: he threw out the lifeline I craved. Had I been to art college, he enquired. I hadn't. 'Good. They think the world owes them a living,' he replied, with a grin. I worked solidly for his agency for the next twenty years.

In the early days I combined this work with another job. Things were that tight. For months I worked every day as a delivery driver for the Royal Woolwich Arsenal Cooperative Society. This involved driving quite a large box van around south-east London delivering bulk purchases like furniture. I remember hauling something heavy up about eight floors of a council tower block on one occasion and being given a cup of tea and a piece of cake by the benevolent old lady concerned.

Most of the night was spent drawing. The whole theory surrounding the drawing of comic strips was still something of a mystery, so it was quite wearing for a while.

I understood some of the basic points quite quickly. Obviously all the movement had to be drawn in such a way as to take the reader's eye along the page to the next frame. At the end of the line the final figure had to face back towards the first picture on the next line of pictures, and so on. To make the whole page more interesting, the individual frames were drawn different sizes, some with broken edges and protruding figures, others with silhouetted figures in a smaller, perhaps even circular, frame with the speech bubbles protruding.

The only reason I had decided to concentrate on comic strips was that they were published weekly.

As the work settled down into a steady stream, I began to think about the long term, especially where to live.

*****

At about this time I saw an advert for a job with the Milk Marketing Board in Cornwall as a milk recorder. I knew about milk recorders and had encountered quite a few over the years. It had always seemed a pretty cushy job to me. Granted it was with cows and I'd vowed never to be involved with them ever again – but at least it didn't include weekends!

I'd always remembered how those Russian linguists, years before, had talked about Cornwall. I'd been to Devon but never over the Tamar. I'd give it a try So I loaded all our worldly goods into the old Austin A30 5cwt van and headed for Truro. There was no road bridge over the Tamar in those days and you crossed by car ferry. Brunel's famous tubular railway bridge towered high up above to the seaward.

By a strange coincidence, when I lived in Truro, Cornwall, my brother Mick lived near Truro, Nova Scotia. By now he was working for the Canadian government on an experimental farm. He used to write occasionally. One memorable letter described the arrival through the swirling midwinter snows of eastern Canada of a group of battered Cadillacs. It was the then relatively unknown Johnny Cash and his entourage. Cash already had a social conscience, apparently, and was performing in a concert in aid of the victims of the infamous mining disaster at Springhill near Amherst. Another fraternal missive described an epic and lonely journey that he undertook when moving from Nova Scotia to Winnipeg out on the prairies of Manitoba. It must have been quite a journey, especially in a battered old VW Beetle in the heat and humidity of a Canadian summer. Apparently he deviated from Nova Scotia into New England and crossed back over the St Lawrence at Kingston, Ontario, heading through Toronto and into the States again at Detroit. Then it was past Saginaw and up over the newly opened Mackinaw bridge at the head of Lake Michigan. It was his description of the next stage of the trip that intrigued me. The southern shore of Lake Superior stretches for some 450 miles and is quite thinly populated. He was amazed to observe small communities still living here in 'tar-paper' huts. This was 1958! I think he was quite pleased to reach Duluth and the final stage to Winnipeg. I forget if he went up through Hibbling, famous, of course, for being the home town of the great Robert Zimmerman. I remember the lines from one of the early songs describing his life in Hibbling as a youth – standing 'at one end of town and being able to see clear through to the other side'. I suppose that sums up what small towns were like in the mid-west at that time.

*****

There followed a year of life in the Duchy, occasionally hard but sometimes idyllic. The two jobs combined well. I had to visit farms twice a day, first in the early morning and second in the late afternoon for the evening milking. Samples of milk were taken from each animal and individual records were brought up to date overnight. The middle of the day was theoretically available to draw comic strips, although because my area was spread over quite an area of Cornwall that middle portion of the day was sometimes unavoidably truncated, but I managed. There

HERODSFOOT / CORNWALL.

were always weekends after all. It was possible in those days to post artwork from the main Truro post office (then, as now, nesting behind the cathedral), at 9.45pm on a

Sunday and it never failed to arrive first thing on Monday morning in Chancery Lane. The postal system was like that almost fifty long years ago.

I felt very much at home in the Duchy. The Cornish folk with whom I came into contact were as I expected they would be. The farming community were the perfect combination of friendliness and independence of spirit. Whether or not it was because I was of farming stock I don't know, but almost all the people I met were warm and welcoming. Most visits ended with an invitation to share their breakfast table. I'd known some areas where this sort of treatment toward a complete stranger would have been laughable.

They lived in such an interesting landscape. A quarter of a mile or so inland for a great swathe along the north coast the stark ruins of mining engine houses were dotted about the countryside, reminding everybody of the harsh conditions under which the Cornish of previous ages had existed. The conditions in the mines must have been horrendous. Very primitive forms of lighting were used and access was by a series of ladders from one shelf to another, down and down. On one particular farm, inland from Holywell Bay, was the grim stone reminder of perhaps the greatest tragedy in Cornish mining history. Although the engine house was quite a distance inland, the mineshaft reached far out under the sea. When the unthinkable happened and the water rushed in, it left one hundred and thirty dead in the dark tunnels. This was not an uncommon occurrence, but this was the worst. Since

being trapped at a tender age in a coffin-like locker in the school gymnasium by a vicious school bully, I have always suffered from claustrophobia. I was there for over an hour, lying on my back with the lid pressed against my face. I think he later became head boy; that was the type which was awarded such positions in those days. Suffering from this phobia as I did, the idea of being below ground in any sort of mine is pretty bad.

On the same farm I remember the farmer pointing out the various inscriptions cut deep into the long beams of his cowshed. They were in Spanish, and certainly looked authentic enough to my questioning eye. He was a genuine old boy and he was convinced that they were graffiti from the time of the Armada, not necessarily from the Armada itself, but more likely spoils of the 'wreckers' that roamed this coast with their decoy lanterns.

Another farmer I visited was the possessor of a good head of pure white hair. He was a jovial thirty-something and seemed to have a completely relaxed attitude to life. Nothing seemed to dent his smiling demeanour. Out of interest one day I asked one of his neighbours aboout him. I wasn't being nosy, but he fascinated me. 'Oh,' said his neighbour, who obviously rated this man pretty highly himself. 'He would never mention it, but his hair turned dead white when he was in the RAF in the war. He was a rear gunner in a Stirling in a raid on Bremen or somewhere, and it was hit by anti-aircraft fire. The plane exploded and he fell out of the rear gun turret at something like fifteen thousand feet, and landed in the mud of the Elbe estuary. Being a Cornishman he was used to a bit of estuary mud and he managed to get out.' I liked that bit.

We heard tales like this during the war, but that must have been a remarkable escape. I could understand his subsequent attitude towards all that life could throw his way. I had an acquaintance who had managed to live through the battle in Burma with the Fourteenth Army and he had that very same attitude. He would say, 'I never for the life of me ever thought I'd get out of the Burmese jungle alive, let alone see the Malvern Hills again, so I'm hardly going to worry about much ever again, am I? Just the family's health, that's all.'

The conditions under which some of the farmers produced their milk worried me for all that. I'd had a little encounter with bovine tuberculosis in my mid-teens so perhaps I was a bit critical of some of the methods I observed. Not that I was sufficiently rewarded for what I did to take on any disciplinary role! One dairy farmer whom I visited regularly lived in a lovely old farmhouse overlooking the Fal. At the entrance to his farm was a large notice informing the world that within this establishment a tuberculin tested herd of South Devons produced the finest milk. On my first visit I was amazed to see him hand-milking in earthen-floored loose boxes. The cows' udders were still covered with dirt and, yes, excrement. I never saw him wash any udders, ever. He would sit and talk incessantly with a cigarette drooping from his lower lip at all times. The ash would fall gently into the foaming bucket, where it would mix with the greenish brown grimy substance that fell occasionally from the palms of his hands. All these ingredients contributed to a remarkable and artistic design in the bucket between his knees. Three cheers for pasteurisation. I would never ever drink milk 'straight from the cow' – but I'd made that decision years previously. As I watched this Cornish farmer at work, I suddenly remembered an exhibition of paintings by Jackson Pollock that I'd seen in Toronto, and recalled that Pollock had been a farmer's son from either Wyoming or Montana. Was this where he got his inspiration for

those gigantic abstract paintings that he conjured up by dripping paint from cans onto a canvas laid on the floor? There was a great similarity.

*****

Another farmer ran an evening cricket team. I turned out for his side whenever I could. Two encounters stick in my mind. One balmy midsummer evening we played at Old Kea. The field was rather narrow and sloped away on all sides, not unlike Laurie Lee's famous Sheepscombe ground high on the Cotswolds near Painswick. It's all a bit hazy after more than forty years, but if I remember correctly the Truro River lay on one side, while the Fal was visible on the other side between the trees below. Behind the bowler's arm, so to speak, lay the widening Fal, Carrick roads and Falmouth. We played for a barrel of beer, I recall. I think we lost, but it was immaterial. The nine gallons soon disappeared. What I do remember is that when we got into our various battered vehicles it became obvious the entire opposition intended to go bass fishing off Falmouth, through the night. It seemed quite a good way to live. Work hard all day, play a game of cricket and then go fishing on a calm and warm sea during a short midsummer night. Nowadays people apparently prefer Playstations!

The other venue was up towards Newquay. We played St Columb on a lovely little ground with a stone wall for a boundary. We batted first and wickets began to fall at the other end.

As one does at such times, I began to chat to their umpire. I remember saying to him, 'Didn't Jack Crapp (of Gloucestershire and England fame) come from somewhere in this part of the world?' He straightened up, swivelled around and pointed to a cottage away beyond the encircling wall. 'His mother used to live in that house over there,' he informed me.

Although it didn't really register at the time, Cornwall had annexed a bit of my soul. Over the years I've paid visits galore to familiar coves and villages, and to paint. But after about a year, one of the wettest they'd ever had, I decided to return to the valley of Severn, to settle in

116

under the Cotswold escarpment and become a fulltime freelance illustrator. It was goodbye to my last real connection with agriculture; cows never again featured in my life. I was still in contact with people in the farming industry and still felt that I was surrounded by countryside, but in reality I no longer had a rural life.

Chapter Nineteen

he first single frame cartoon that I managed to sell to a national publication was, by chance, on an agricultural theme. It was published on the joke page in *TV Times* sometime in 1958. It was quite simple and featured an enraged bull staring out of a TV screen, complete with wild eyes and steam emitting from its nostrils. Around its enormous horns was an array of cables and a swinging microphone. The caption read, 'We apologise for the breakdown in sound from our farming programme . . .'. I think I've seen worse.

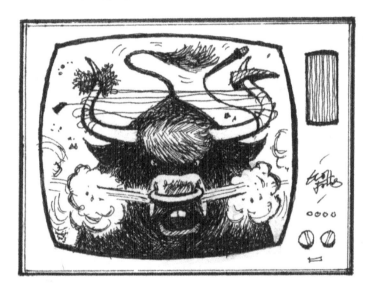

Over the next twenty years I drew realistic picture stories for almost fifty different publications, ranging from *Film Fun* to *TV Century 21* from *Boys' World* to *Lion* and *Swift*, *Valiant* and *Victor*, as well as a great variety of picture stories for girls' publications, such as *Judy*, *Sally* and *School Friend*, *Penelope*, *Jackie* and many more – much to the embarrassment of my teenage son. Does anyone remember 'The Jet Skaters' in *Lion* or 'Fay Farrell – District Nurse' in *Judy*? [

I suppose I ought to go into greater detail about those two decades. The first job that I ever did was for the *London Mystery Magazine*. I can't remember what on earth it was about. For a while I drew picture stories for Mick Anglo's studios in Gower Street. He was the man who brought 'Marvelman' comics to Britain. Apparently only a few months before both Bob Monkhouse and Denis Goodwin had worked there for him. I recall that Monkhouse was quite critical of Mick in his autobiography. I can only think that friend Monkhouse had a rather exalted opinion of his own talents, for I liked Mick Anglo.

In the early days I drew a regular strip that was featured on the front and back of *TV Fun* and featured happenings in the life of Dickie Henderson and Anthea Askey – based on a popular sitcom of the time. Many of the other strips that I drew were stories of contemporary pop music personalities, for publications such as *Roxy*, *Mirabelle*, *Valentine* and the like. I can't say that I was even slightly interested in what so-called celebrities did or thought, but it was reasonably well paid and the warmth of a studio in midwinter compared favourably with memories of mud, cow-muck and kale-cutting.

Later I spent all my days and lots of nights drawing picture adventure strips for children's comics. I remember thinking that I'd almost made it when I drew a few episodes of 'Blackbow the Cheyenne' in *Swift*. This was part of the Hulton Press and was known as the younger person's *Eagle*. I also drew in some *Girl* annuals (this was a sister paper of the *Eagle*). My over-confidence was quickly deflated, however,when Hulton Press suddenly ceased to exist, and it was back to grinding out tales for the people in Dundee and Farringdon Street.

In 1974 I attended a comic strip weekend convention at a hotel near Marble Arch. The idea was to celebrate the hundredth anniversary of the first comic strip character 'Ally Sloper'. I remember being very surprised to see Mick Anglo sitting apparently alone at the bar. I hadn't seen him for seventeen years and stepped diffidently up beside him, saying, 'You won't remember me . . . er . . .'. He grinned, punched me in the chest, and said, "Course I remember you, you bloody idiot. What're you drinking?' By coincidence Bob Monkhouse was the guest of honour at the big event of the weekend. He was the complete opposite of the vision that assailed us daily on our television screens. Perhaps he knew he was among a pretty hard-bitten audience; who knows. It was quite a do. Everybody I'd ever heard of seemed to be there, including a very frail-looking Frank Hampson, world famous as the creator of Dan Dare.

He was, by now, unable to draw any more and was eking out a living as a night-watchman at the meteorological centre at Bracknell. It was rumoured at about this time that the firm that owned and published Dan Dare was selling original Frank Hampson boards for around £250 a time. The head of the firm concerned, who was speaking on some subject or other, received a great deal of raucous flack. It was good to see and hear. I had been placed at a table with some quite famous people, including the great Steve Dowling, who began Garth in the *Mirror*, and many other famous strips. He was so gracious and lacking in conceit. I remember how surprised he was when people came up to pester him for autographs. He just looked mystified and murmured, 'Why?'

*****

In the early seventies I became a member of the Cartoonists' Club of Great Britain and enjoyed many hours of convivial company in a variety of locations. There were regular meetings at the Cartoonist pub just off Fleet Street and entertaining experiences at, for example, Birmingham and Cardiff, and the annual convention at Pwllhelli. These people seemed just as amusing as they were on the printed page.

I remember Bill Tidy making a very dramatic appearance at Pwllhelli. It was early dawn, midsummer, and we'd spent the final night around a huge bonfire down near the water's edge. Mist was swirling across Tremadoc Bay, and Snowdon was slowly appearing against a pink dawn. It was all quite ethereal. Suddenly, far off, and almost as if walking on water, came this tall figure clad in a flowing white sheet, with right arm upraised. As he came nearer we could hear a hectoring voice ranting against the evils of the demon drink and the temptations of the flesh. Stopping at about thirty paces distant, Bill continued the most lucid and almost unnerving lecture. It was all completely impromptu. Then he stretched to his full six feet four inches, swept the sheet over his shoulder dramatically, exclaiming 'And for my next trick . . .', and strode back to the swirling mists.

There were others, such as Terry Parkes ('Larry'), Chic Jacob, Les Lilley, Clive Collins, Gren Jones and, of course, my long-time friend, Mike Atkinson. Some years later Mike and I arranged a day out for the club at Cheltenham Races. Many of them came down and had a truly memorable weekend. Edward Gillespie arranged a box for us high in the grandstand, demanding only that every cartoonist would supply a relevant cartoon to be displayed permanently in the Prestbury Park gallery.

I am glad to have known them all.

*****

By 1978 I realised that comics were in a steep decline. They paid the same amount per page as they had done in 1957, which was bad news. It was also at this time that my marriage finally disintegrated. After all we'd been through it was a sad episode, but the stresses of being a freelance probably didn't help.

Chapter Twenty

For a couple of years in the late seventies I drew a weekly strip in *Reveille*, called 'Hey Penny', in collaboration with the famous comic art historian the late Denis Gifford.

But as usual another door opened and I went off to the big city again to enroll with an agency that specialised in the drawing of storyboards. They were mainly for television commercials and short films. It was very much like drawing comic strips, only in full colour and for about ten times the money. But the work was very wearing for all that: there was little let-up. The usual routine was roughly this: I'd get a phone call and a faxed script in the afternoon, would work all night, and would then take the twenty-odd frames up to London by eight or nine o'clock the next morning. This entailed a thirty-five mile dash by car to Swindon at about 6am, a train to Paddington and then tube to the West End. The hour-long journey to Paddington enabled me to catch up on a bit of sleep, on the principle that the train went no further than the terminus. This was usually all plain sailing, but there were occasions when I'd dash into some world-famous agency and present my drawings only to be rewarded, smilingly and apologetically, with, 'oh yes they're fine, but we've decided to change the ending. . . . There's a studio you can use down there. If there's anything you need, like magic markers, just shout. Can I get you a cup of coffee?'

On more than one occasion I would spend all day 'in house' drawing a different end sequence, dash back to Paddington, fall into a Swindon-bound train and fall asleep, only to wake as the express pulled into Bath station. It was another hour before there was a train back to Swindon, where I was reunited with my old MGB GT, and I'd be home in time to fall into bed. Strangely enough, by then I'd be fully awake and sleep would be fitful or non-existent.

When I first joined them Storyboards Ltd were in Long Acre. Over the years they moved first to Tavistock Street in Covent Garden and later to Greek Street in Soho. Among the five hundred and more storyboard sequences that I produced over the following twelve years were many for adverts that were used for quite long periods on the TV screen. In the early days they were usually fifteen to twenty frames in length. Frames were anything from 5in x 4in upwards. They were always in full colour, which was applied by magic markers or pantones. I could never really understand why they had to be in such detail and so 'finished' in appearance. They were shown by the agency to the prospective clients and were then binned. That is quite difficult to take as, by today's standards, these bits of original artwork could fetch a lot of money. It amazed me that a client couldn't just read the script and imagine what the end product would look like. But why argue? There was a lot of money changing hands

Later there were many more 'animatics', which were made up into rather basic short animated film sequences. Some were extremely complicated. You had to draw large backgrounds and very many cut-out figures and objects. I remember being the illustrator for the launch of the Ford Sierra in the spring of 1982. A television studio was hired by J.Walter Thompson for some three days (including the two nights!) and a famous Madison Avenue director was hired for the shoot. I remember the apprehension in those studios as we awaited his arrival: whispers of 'He's landed at Heathrow!', and so on. When he did materialise it was something of a shock. Apparently he was known as 'The Duke' and subconsciously I had envisaged a John Wayne figure, all six foot four of him. But the man who arrived was five foot nothing, stocky, with a classic West Point crewcut. Not at all flamboyant, he hardly uttered a word to the crew other than 'Cut' and was a generally calming presence. He couldn't have been more gracious to me. I'd drawn many large background shots of typically Mediterranean coastal road scenes – in and out of tunnels, over bridges, the lot. These were placed on to the screens of various TV sets about the studio. They would then shoot the cutouts against a strange green background, and these images would then appear on larger television screens as if they were part of the whole thing. It was quite impressive.

Obviously the car had to be drawn in about twenty-five different poses, at different angles, together with lots of people in various positions. Occasionally they needed a shot at a slightly different angle. The director would step over and say, 'Geoffrey, could I have just one more shot at this or that angle,' tap me on the shoulder encouragingly, then light up the enormous cigar that seemed to be a permanent fixture.

I'd been on my feet for almost sixty hours by the time we actually finished. The great man ambled over, put his arm round my weary shoulders and thanked me profusely for my efforts. To my astonishment he insisted on getting me a taxi in which to return to Paddington, said '*Au revoir*', and waved as he made his departure. It was yet another reminder that some people in positions of authority can behave with kindness and dignity.

I found the advertising agency fraternity almost without exception to be totally unlike the bombastic posers depicted on television or in films. There were a few, of course, who talked rather loudly about their impending weekend in the 'Med', but they were few and far between. They seemed to work extremely long hours, rather like the agricultural communities that I'd known so well in an earlier life. I suppose that if you didn't come up with the goods you were out, as it was a creative industry. It was as basic as that, perhaps.

The subjects were so varied that it is pointless to try and remember even a cross-section. I seemed to specialise in new car launches, including (as well as the Ford Sierra) the Renault 18. The making of this ad became a complete programme for the late night Sunday programme *The South Bank Show*. It wasn't strictly accurate, I recall. There were advertisements for new foods, publications, insurance companies, beers, banks, everything. I also drew quite a few short storyboards for Department of the Environment films. Sometimes, as I worked away in these internationally famous ad agencies, I would look around as these industrious people dashed about, some of them quite famous in the industry, and I'd think, I wonder what these sophisticates would say if I told them that long ago I'd ploughed with horses, milked thirty-five cows twice a day, thatched corn ricks and so on. I imagined their reaction would be amazement, and perhaps just a little condescension. Fifteen, twenty years later I think I might have been pleasantly surprised. Perhaps they would have been interested.

One of the most famous creative directors of the last quarter century, the recently deceased John Webster of Boase Massimi & Pollitt, was someone who really was very interested in things rural. In the early eighties I storyboarded a great many of his ideas and grew to like him very much. He was extremely kind and attentive, and seemed to love to talk about the real world outside the metropolis. Reading through the extensive broadsheet obituaries devoted to him, I learned that on retirement he bought a vineyard and kept his many friends supplied with wine.

*****

Sometime in the eighties I was sent off with Alan Austin (who used to run the Association of Illustrators), to Lexington Street to RSA films, for whom I'd done a few DTI short film storyboards. To my surprise we were shown in to see Ridley Scott himself. He proposed making a film of Frank Herbert's famous sci-fi epic *Dune*. Not being a sci-fi buff I hadn't read the book. I'd heard of it, of course, but I felt a bit wary. Ridley Scott himself was a rather stern red-haired Geordie. The amazing thing about that meeting was that he brought out some of the most spectacular artwork I've ever seen. He'd apparently done it himself! 'This is the sort of thing I want,' he informed us. Alan and I exchanged surreptitious glances, but both said we were ready for it. We left those studios, each clutching an eight hundred page edition of *Dune* and wondering what the future held. I came home and read a couple of hundred pages. It was all about giant worms in a sandy desert landscape, and did nothing at all for me. I began to get a little apprehensive about the whole project. Imagine my relief when Storyboard-Harpers rang to inform me that the project was on hold as Ridley Scott had suddenly gone off to Hollywood. He never did make *Dune*. He left it to David Lynch, who had his own storyboard artists.

The creative directors seemed to be extremely attentive and kind towards the people on whom they relied. Perhaps I didn't see the tantrums that are alleged to occur. Perhaps they relied on the people like me, who made their ideas a reality overnight - literally. I never thought of it like that, but was always pleasantly relieved that I'd got it more or less how they'd imagined it to be. Early on I was often quietly amused by their reactions to the artwork that I provided. They would say things like, 'Don't you get a lot of movement into each frame? It's more than we usually get.

Have you ever thought of drawing comic strips?' These were people in the higher echelons of internationally famous advertising agencies like J. Walter Thompson, Ogilvie and Mather, Saatchis and the like. I would smile, thanking them for the compliment, and change the subject. These people were forking out fees of which I had never dreamed as I scratched away endlessly at episodes of 'Paddy McGinty's Goat', 'Fay Farrell – District Nurse', 'The Jet Skaters' and so on. They were right; it was very much like drawing action adventure stories. Occasionally the stories in the comics and the storyboards would be about rural life, and I could indulge myself completely. I remember drawing an ad sequence about a rural wedding, putting in an extra frame in which a passing tractor and muckspreader roared past just as the bride emerged – bits of cow muck flying everywhere. They kept it in the TV ad, which appealed to my vanity.

*****

Strangely, being confronted by a large page of blank white paper is not unlike driving a tractor and plough through the gate into a field of stubble. For a moment it's a bit daunting, but once you've made the first lines, marking out your intentions, then it all falls into place.

In the early nineties computers began to be used in the studios of advertising agencies. I suppose it was simpler to download a background scene and another of people in roughly appropriate positions. Freelance illustrators became a bit of an irrelevance.

129

Chapter Twenty-One

*O*ver the years, especially in the decades in which I churned out endless picture stories, my link with normality was playing club cricket. During those years various amusing and memorable things occurred that were in stark contrast to the usual cricketing encounters depicted in fiction and especially on stage. We've all seen the scenes of hearty blazered fools and rural boneheads engaged in some unrecognisable farce. I suppose the Hampstead set lap it up, but nobody who's ever played would give it the time of day. Two of the memories that spring to mind concern occasions on which I succumbed to the first ball of the match, so there's no self-aggrandisement here I hope.

Not only the first ball of the match, one of these instances concerned the first ball of the season. Pershore often opened their season against Banbury, and this particular year it was away at Banbury. A cold wind was blowing across the exposed field, bringing with it just a faint smell of coffee grains from the nearby General Foods factory. I rushed there thinking I was late, but amazingly I was one of the first to arrive. After a while a coin was tossed and Sid Fudger, our skipper, elected to bat. He had little choice as only about half a dozen of our team had shown up by that time. Years before, for other teams in other places, I'd opened the innings on frequent occasions. But this team had its regularly high scoring batsmen to fill the first five places. I had become a specialist number seven batsman: people will understand the phrase. 'You might as well open,' I was told by the captain, who had an eye perpetually fixed on the distant gateway.

Soon we had an almost complete team. In any case we had enough to start with as we were taking first knock. The opening bowler was well known to us. He was a belligerent Yorkshireman and I had once heard him say 'I hate batsmen', repeating one of Fred Trueman's intellectual comments. He was a fast left armer who'd 'played a lot in th' leagues, tha knows', and incidentally for Oxfordshire in the Minor Counties competition. He bounded up, I played forward defensively, missed and was dismayed to hear the familiar rattle behind me. The effect on our friend was amazing. He yelled and shouted, leapt high in the air, punched his fist like a victorious pugilist and looked as if he was about to deliver a tirade of derogatory comments. The route back to the pavilion lay (unusually), past the other set of wickets. Making that walk I had time to think of something to say. Eyes blazing with triumph, he turned towards me as I approached. Before he could utter a word I said, 'I rather gather you don't take many in the course of a season.' Members of his own team behind him were chuckling away and one even gave a little clap and a wink.

In mid-season we played the return match at Pershore. It's a long time ago now, but I seem to remember that I had broken a finger – or it might just have been another loss of form. Anyway, I'd volunteered to be official umpire. I've always quite liked umpiring. As a specialist number seven or eight batsman, it's something at which you get quite experienced. Bowling from my end, our friend opened their attack again. As usual he appealed for everything. After his third unsuccessful appeal he began to get abusive as he passed. Two or three overs later he appealed for an LBW, for a ball that had pitched about a foot outside the leg stump. As he was bowling left arm over the wicket and as it had cut back quite a way, the ball would probably had hit middle and off. But there was no way it was out. He burst into a furious tirade, full of the most colourful expletives. This was quite soon after soccer referees began to show dissident players coloured cards as warnings. Knowing that I would be umpiring I had had an inkling this would occur, and I had come prepared. I stepped to one side, took a yellow card from my breast pocket and showed it to all four corners of the ground. He didn't swear again all afternoon.

The other first ball duck was on what used to be a Gloucestershire county venue at Lydney.

I'd worked all night finishing off a three-page picture story that had to be in on Monday morning. It was Sunday, and I posted off the artwork in Kings Square in Gloucester as I drove through. Arriving at Lydney, I felt more like lying down on the grass and sleeping than playing cricket. There had been a rare mix-up by the

Lydney fixture secretary. Unfortunately as we arrived so did Thornbury. (Playing for them, to our amazement, was a Dr Grace replete in multi-coloured blazer.) Red faces were in evidence, but being English and polite the Lydney team had no real option other than to sit and watch. The Lydney captain that day was Peter James, whose son Steve later played for Glamorgan and for England. As everything was somewhat chaotic and I'd had weeks without even getting to the crease, I was surprised to be invited to open the innings. It was too good an opportunity to miss, even if I was near to collapse with lack of sleep. Of course, before I could concentrate my mind I was back in the pavilion. First ball, the clattering woodwork again. For all that, I remember it as being a unique match: it ended in a tie, 181 each.

Some years later Pershore played Ross-on-Wye on a lovely September day at Pershore.

The Ross players arrived in a very confident mood. It had been their good fortune in mid-season to obtain the services of Gloucestershire's Barbadian, Wycliffe Phillips. Nobody knew why he'd abruptly left the county as he was at the top of their batting averages. But we also knew the feudal system down in Bristol, so it was no surprise. Ross had won every game since Wycliffe had joined them and they had great delight in telling us that he'd got an average of 247 for them! They obviously thought it was going to be easy, for a change. Batting first, Ross opened with Wycliffe Phillips at number one. I was fielding at second slip. Our opening fast bowler Pete Seward came roaring in from the fruit market end. There was a strange unleashing of power, mid-off leapt skywards as the ball scorched past his unprotected ankles, and there was a crack as the ball hit the wall in front of the fruit market, rebounding almost all the way back to the square. It was a stroke full of Caribbean power and grace. A truly marvellous shot. John Bomford at first slip turned to me and said, 'Christ, if he gets an edge we're in dead trouble.' We both retreated a further fifteen feet. The bowler charged in. The shot appeared to be a repeat of the first, only its sound was different. In a split-second I realised that there was a black blur heading straight at my skull. I instinctively raised my left hand in self-defence, luckily palm outward, and ducked!

I was beginning to fall over backwards. Suddenly I was aware that the ball was deep in my left hand: the force must have closed the fingers. Suddenly there was a lot of cheering and I realised that I'd actually caught it, completely by accident. Wycliffe Phillips himself, in a moment of supreme sportsmanship, was smiling broadly. He even laughed when one of the Pershore close fielders, Neville Lewis, put an arm around his shoulders and said, 'I think it's racial prejudice, Wycliffe, 'cos he's dropped everything else all season.' I hadn't, but it sounded funny. We won.

OWZAT!

Chapter Twenty-Two

arly in 1988 I was lucky enough to win, in an art-related competition, two air tickets to anywhere in the USA. It would make a change from Cornwall, we mused. By now my life was shared with Andrea, who became my wife. In her I think I have been incredibly lucky, and although there is a considerable age difference we seem to have arrived at a position of mutual affection and respect. Having graduated in psychology from Manchester, she later became a chartered librarian and has devoted her life to books and, thankfully, looking after and encouraging me. I am eternally grateful to her.

I spent that summer working flat out, storyboarding. In the sixteen days leading up to our departure I drew over 100 storyboard frames in full colour. The result was that I was shattered before we started. It wasn't a clever thing to doBut if we were going to have a really memorable holiday it would probably cost quite a lot,

even if the air travel was to be free. As I'd already been to New England the obvious thing was to get tickets for the west coast and San Francisco. This was arranged for mid-September, so we would have the most pleasant weather.

Off from Gatwick, across the pond, down the eastern seaboard and across to Houston. It was, I remember, over 100°F in Houston. Then on to the City on

UNION SQUARE, SAN FRANCISCO / LOOKING NORTH ON POWELL.

the Bay. The pilot announced that to give us a treat he would divert slightly so we could all get a view of the Grand Canyon from the air. Everybody moved to the one side of the airplane. There were cries in jest on the intercom of 'other side the ship!' I recall.

After almost a day's sleep we set out to enjoy San Francisco. The whole two and a half weeks were magical. We did the obvious touristy things like a trip round the bay, out under the Golden Gate Bridge, a close look at Alcatraz, a wander round Chinatown, rides on the street cars and all the things that were expected of visitors. We were predictable. After a few days we hired a car and headed south, down to Half Moon Bay, apparently 'the pumpkin capital of the world', and on down the coastal highway to Santa Cruz, with its boardwalk, then to Monterey. It was great to find Steinbeck's 'Cannery Row' there, cleaned up and not smelling of fish at all. We stayed in that area for a while in a nice motel, and went to Pacific Grove, Cypress Point, Pebble Beach and the Seventeen-Mile Drive to Carmel: we did it all. I sat on the empty sands of Fantail Beach and painted a quick watercolour – collecting a few

CARMEL/CALIF '88

onlookers, which I never really enjoy. At Carmel we went to Clint Eastwood's restaurant, The Hog's Breath. Clint wasn't there, of course, but it was quite an impressive establishment. In the barnyard area of Carmel I came upon a large gallery full of paintings of the western states by famous artists, which was a pleasant experience. One day we drove up the Salinas Valley: more Steinbeck country. It was like paying homage. Then we were off down the magnificent coastal road south, over the famous Bixby Bridge and on, past Henry Miller's library and into Jack Kerouac country, Big Sur.

We were so captivated by Big Sur that we stayed there for many days, living in a log cabin in the hills and going down to the raging surf during the days. We discovered Nepenthe, a spectacular cantilevered restaurant perched in the rocks, four hundred and fifty feet above the booming ocean. It had been built by Frank Lloyd Wright as a wedding present from Orson Welles to Rita Hayworth, only she didn't like it! Later it had been converted into a famous eating place. It was the ideal place for an evening meal. Although late September it was still quite warm. Despite this, in the evening there was an open wood fire in the centre of the restaurant, with the windows open, Mexican wind chimes and a full moon shining on the Pacific way below. It was truly memorable.

We had intended to go on to San Simeon, Randolph Hearst's castle, but we just stayed in Big Sur. I was weary anyway. Eventually we headed back towards San Francisco, staying for a few nights in a luxurious motel in the middle of the Hansel and Gretel area of Carmel. Then back for a few days beside the bay, a trip over the Golden Gate to Sausalito, Muir Woods and beyond. At last I saw some full size sequoias, over three hundred feet high.

We had originally planned to venture way above San Francisco if we had time – but I suppose that was a crazy idea. We had both always loved the Kate and Anna McGarrigle song 'Talk to me of Mendicino', and it was up there on the coast, past the bay that Hitchcock used for *The Birds*. As we knew the path down to Polridmouth in Cornwall that had apparently given Daphne Du Maurier the idea for the original story, it would have been nice to have seen the American location as well, but that's life.

It was rather strange the way that California seemed somehow to be connected to my musical memories. Going through Santa Cruz I immediately thought of Ry Cooder, having seen a film of him in concert on the boardwalk (and also live on more than one occasion in England). I've always had a partiality towards American guitar virtuosos. Besides Ry Cooder, whom I regard as a genius, I've long been an aficionado of Leo Kottke. I have a CD on which, among all the Americana, he plays a very slow and haunting rendition of Bach's 'Jesu, Joy of Man's Desiring'. Many people try to play it much too quickly, I feel. (I seem to remember Scott Joplin's dictum was to play ragtime as slowly as was humanly possible – and this seems appropriate with a lot of other music too.) Once at a literary festival we were listening with great interest to the memories of Garrison Keillor. To my astonishment he recounted that in his early days he used to retire to an isolated farm in rural Minnesota and always put on some Leo Kottke, as he was the perfect accompaniment to his thoughts. In Monterey the image of the legendary Otis Redding came straight into my thoughts, with the memory of his marvellous rendition of 'I've been loving you too long', which was performed at Monterey in 1966, I seem to remember. I suppose these feelings were accentuated in Monterey because in our motel were many jazz musicians who were playing at the 1988 festival. Somehow that music of the sixties and seventies always sounds to me as if it's coming in off the pounding surf. Bands like the Flying Burrito Brothers and the Byrds come to mind.

Eventually it was all over. As the aircraft headed east over the Sacramento Valley I was congratulating myself on getting a seat next to a window, when I began to get requests to draw the curtain so that people could watch an old film – when so much of interest lay below us! I couldn't believe it. Down below we passed over the Great Salt Lake, the Mormon township and on over the beginnings of the High Sierras and the Rockies. The first snows of winter were clearly visible. But at last a steward insisted that I watched the film like everybody else. Soon we were landing in Newark: it seemed amazing that we'd crossed the entire continent. Perhaps I'd slept. An hour or two's rather disturbing wait to repair an engine, and it was off into the night above the lights of New York City. A sleep, and then down below were the Cliffs of Moher, the Irish Sea, the Bristol Channel and, in a few minutes, the south coast of England. England seems so tiny after North America.

Chapter Twenty-Three

The adventure was over. It was back to the harsh reality of endless storyboards. By the millennium most things had changed, and I was mainly doing illustration work for educational publications, interspersed with watercolours, landscapes, seascapes - anything that might sell! I had a successful exhibition locally, but mainly it was originals and prints that sold in a west country gallery (the Wesley House Gallery in Polperro), as well as prints all over the world via my website.

During the nineties I did various bits of artwork for some of the Gloucestershire cricketers, including Andy Stovold, the great Courtney Walsh and their one-day cricket wizard, Mark Alleyne: montages of their careers, that sort of thing. Later came commissions for test players Mike Smith and Steve James of Glamorgan.

It was probably as a result of this, and thanks to the recommendation of Chris Coley (influential in the set-up down at Bristol), that in May 1999 I was invited to take part in a special one-off edition of Channel 4's successful television series *Watercolour Challenge*. They chose three professional artists to paint a cricket match on the Gloucestershire county ground at the King's School in Gloucester. The confrontation was between Mark Alleyne's Glos XI and David English's famous charity side, the Bunbury's, which included celebrities like Stephen Tompkinson, Leslie Grantham, Michael Nyman and ex-steeplechase jockey Peter Scudamore. The other two contestants were Jocelyn Goldsworthy, often to be seen on test match television coverage busily painting away at the boundary edge, and Rob Perry, a sporting portraitist and Free Forester cricketer. The weather was appalling – not that it rained very much, but it was as cold as many a day in midwinter. We were covered in rugs and hot water bottles, and hot drinks were supplied liberally. We had only four hours in which to paint the scene. That was the theory. In effect we arrived at about half past nine and were there until eight o'clock in the evening, but I doubt if any of us managed four hours of actual painting. There were interviews, shoots and re-shoots and a break for lunch up in the city. Even so, it was a very pleasant experience. The television crew couldn't have been more helpful or pleasant. Hannah Gordon, who was the commère of the series, was wonderful. She was kind, friendly and completely devoid of any thespian vanity. As far as I was concerned the weather won! It eroded almost all sense of competition. Young Rob Perry was adjudged the winner, and deservedly so. The judge, incidentally, was Gloucestershire's own cricketer artist (in every sense), wicket keeper Jack Russell. I remember driving home and lying in a hot bath for ages. I hadn't felt so cold since those far-off days of kale cutting and sprout picking.

Also in the late nineties I was asked by Edward Gillespie, controller of everything at Prestbury Park, to be one of half a dozen artists to contribute a mural to decorate the walls of the newly constructed betting hall at Cheltenham Racecourse. Mine was in the shape of a twelve foot wide 'page' of comic strip, in full colour, relating to a day at the races. I enjoyed doing it, but every time I go to the races I nip down to see if it's still there – and always go away dissatisfied. It's the thought that I could have done it so much better. I suppose that's a natural reaction: it's how artists improve their technique.

*****

I began to receive emails from distant parts, with correspondents requesting prints of places that had figured far back in their forefathers' lives. A good proportion of these were Cornish scenes – as the Cornish exported their mining skills to all parts of the globe, especially the Antipodes, South Africa and above all North America. (An obvious sporting connection is Bob Fitzsimmons back in Edwardian times, always quoted as Britain's first world heavyweight champion. He was apparently a Cornishman from the mining area of far-off Nevada.) Some years ago I received an email from a lady in Greenboro', North Carolina. She wanted to purchase a print of a painting that I had done years before of the picturesque village of Lerryn, near Lostwithiel. It's a lovely spot, with an old packhorse bridge over the river Lerryn. There's a pub nearby, and stepping stones across the stream. Apparently, a decade earlier she'd been in England and visited Lerryn – and had been so impressed with the place that some time later she had named her daughter after the village. It was a lovely story, and I was only too pleased to send the print winging across the Atlantic.

More recently I read Bill Bryson's early book describing a trip around his native land, *The Lost Continent.* In his travels he arrived in the mining area down by the far end of Lake Superior in Minnesota, near to Duluth, or was it Hibbling? There he purchased the worst Cornish pasty he'd ever tasted.

One of the many Cornish scenes I've painted was of the ocean's edge at low tide at Polzeath, close to the mouth of the Camel Estuary and the idyllic Daymer Bay at Trebetherick, so beloved by the poet John Betjeman. He's actually buried in that strange little church lying deep in the golf course, with its gnarled and twisted remnant of a spire. Apparently the church was completely buried in the sand for over a hundred years; well, that's how legend has it. The Polzeath print has been a bestseller via my website. The story of its origin is quite interesting. We were on holiday in September 2001. It was Monday 10th, the day before the world was changed by a group of demented religious bigots, probably yelling the universal call of 'yah, boo, my god's better than your god!' But there I go again, showing my inability to countenance any organised dogma. But it's true, I think: without religion there would be few wars and the world would be a much better place. We'd spent a lazy afternoon parked in the field at Daymer Bay, reading the *Guardian* and the *Independent*, occasionally snoozing in the late summer sun, gazing down the wide expanse of sand towards the distant roofs of Padstow. At about six o'clock we decided to make our way back to base in Polperro. But first we would head north a few miles to Polzeath. It had been years since we had been there. Usually quite crowded, Polzeath was almost deserted and the tide was way out. Parking the car on the firm dry sand we set out to walk the two or three hundred yards to the booming surf and the cry of the gulls. It was magical, still quite warm, with Stepper Point a blue hazy silhouette over to the left and Pentire Head looming up on the right. A few hardy surfers were still enjoying themselves. This was Cornwall as I remembered it from long ago, out of peak season, almost deserted. No screaming crowds, and the kids all back at school. The peace of this reverie was shattered by the clanging of a bell close behind, and we were overtaken by the local Mr Softee van – who proceeded to dispense ice cream to the surfers (and to us), and tootled off towards the distant houses. I took a few photos, and later that year came up with a painting that seemed to more or less capture the scene that day. Much later I read somewhere that the poet Laurence Binyon, who wrote the elegy to the First World War dead 'Lest we forget', actually wrote it sitting on those rocks looking out to sea. I wonder if it was at the going down of the sun. In view of what happened the day after we were there, it seems a fitting postscript to the folly of mankind.

*****

Late in 2004 I decided to do a painting from memory of the old homestead that had played such a dominant part in my early life. I eventually arrived at the correct viewpoint and began to draw. In its final form it's quite a lot bigger than I had originally intended. Concentrating on just the farmhouse, buildings and surrounding yards I began a very detailed representation. A strange feeling overwhelmed me. I could remember every bush – although I didn't necessarily include them. As I drew I began to remember international news that had occurred all those decades before. It became quite spooky. Eventually I completed the painting. Looking at smaller prints of it now, everything looks remarkably tidy, devoid of detritus, no mud anywhere. It was obviously late summer, to excuse myself. There was undoubtedly a cathartic effect in what I had done. This was further enhanced after I took the framed painting to the present owner for him to see. After our very pleasant and kind reception, and a tour of the premises, I felt as if I'd closed a chapter of my life. He insisted on purchasing the original, which was pleasing.

Church Farm · Queenhill · Worcs

I suppose that through much of my life as a
freelance illustrator I have dreamed of eventually
purchasing a smallholding in picturesque countryside,

probably within sight of the ocean in Cornwall. I would keep a few sheep and fowls and convert one of the buildings into a comfortable roomy studio, with perhaps a pottery studio to complete the daydream. Life isn't like that as a one-man freelance, of course. Eventually, though, you realise just how lucky you have been to earn a living for almost fifty years just by the output from one hand.

As I approach the end of this book I realise there's no mention of my having any interest in art or even any artistic leaning until I reached the time when a decision had to be made regarding a career change – when that motorway was on the horizon. I certainly never thought of being a full-time artist until that time in late '56 when we were leaving the farm for ever. Lack of capital removed any hope of being a farmer again, and I had no intention of being a glorified labourer on someone else's farm. Reason, or perhaps lack of it, suggested that I might possibly be able to draw well enough to do it professionally. I recalled that fellow National Servicemen in the Intelligence Corps had opined that I had sufficient natural talent. But in the intervening two years or so since demobilisation I doubt I'd drawn anything at all. It had been two years of concentrated slog to get Jones Bros up and running as a business – all to no avail, thanks to the Ministry of Transport.

I've tried to think of some sign, however minute, in my early life of what pushed me in the direction I eventually headed. There is one tiny clue. When I was eight or nine years old I entered a painting competition in the *Farmer & Stockbreeder*, and promptly forgot all about it. I doubt if I even told anybody about it. One day the postman brought an unexpected parcel, and it transpired that I had won first prize. There, emerging from the discarded brown paper, was a large Winsor and Newton painting set. It was quite a sophisticated piece of equipment. Not many years ago I still had that box, but sadly I can't remember ever having put its contents to much use. I have a very distant, valued, memory of my father being proud of my success in that competition, although sadly I have very few memories that indicate whether he considered what life might have in store for his two sons. I suspect he hoped we might be spared the endless grinding toil that agriculture can so easily become – and he must have hoped we would be spared the horrors to which his own generation had been subjected. There is another memory, of hearing him describe my inordinately long fingers as 'artist's hands'. I was so young at the time that it passed from my mind and has only resurfaced as I pen these lines. In any case those hands were soon to be widened and coarsened with years of manual toil, in winter usually cracked, chapped and bleeding.

I've come to the inevitable conclusion that the craft of illustration is almost entirely based on observation. The representation of realistic images is a relatively simple matter of transferring your observed perceptions onto paper. In this respect, I suppose I was entirely self-taught. I merely observed the manner in which people moved and the way that perspective worked. It was all there in front of my eyes. Of course it would have been very useful to have received some tuition, but that was never likely to be forthcoming in the depths of rural Worcestershire.

I suppose that what little extra knowledge I acquired was as a result of reading. By that I most certainly do not mean ploughing through endless manuals devoted to how to draw. It was more a case of being interested in the work of famous illustrators and painters. I can't really claim to have studied the work of the great painters of earlier centuries. My interest lay in the various schools of painting that have emerged since the middle of the nineteenth century: the Pre-Raphaelites, Impressionists, post-Impressionists, the Norwich School, the Glasgow Boys and the Newlyn School. Most of the images produced by previous centuries seemed to be concerned with religious subjects, which I regarded as fantasy anyway.

People have suggested that the army was significant in my becoming an illustrator. Actually I think the opposite was true. The army merely used my existing talent for their own use, and at very little cost. They taught me absolutely nothing, apart from a detestation of the glorification of slaughtering other human beings. I have little doubt that I would have attempted to become an illustrator after being deprived of my planned livelihood, quite apart from that soul-destroying part of my life spent in khaki. Even so, I suppose there was one way in which those two years influenced my decision about the future.

147

After the stultifying experience of National Service and the ignominy that I endured at the behest of infantile minds misusing their authority, the idea of being self-employed in a creative industry was very appealing. Obviously there are other forms of art that are in many ways more interesting, more prestigious and economically rewarding.

To be honest I feel honoured to have been able to live such a life. Perhaps the experience of being an unwilling conscript at such a vital time of my life, the sheer boring waste of it, made me see the following years in a completely different light. As well, of course, I've met many interesting people with whom I would never otherwise have come into contact.

Farming has left its legacy in another way. All those early years of being soaked through every day during endless winters, combined with the odd sporting mishap, has ensured that for the past decade I have become progressively very arthritic, just like most of the farmer's sons who were my contemporaries. Still, it's been a life I wouldn't exchange, not any of it at any price.

But now it's back to the drawing board. . . .

.

Lightning Source UK Ltd.
Milton Keynes UK
UKOW07f1328161214

243237UK00001B/11/P